P9-DEL-405

WAPITI
WILDERNESS

Margaret and Olaus Murie, 1959

WAPITI WILDERNESS

BY

Margaret & Olaus Murie

With pen-and-ink drawings by Olaus Murie

COLORADO ASSOCIATED UNIVERSITY PRESS

Copyright © 1985 by Margaret E. Murie
Published by Colorado Associated University Press
Boulder, Colorado 80309
ISBN 0-87081-155-x
Library of Congress Catalog Card Number 65-18767
Printed in the United States of America
Originally published in 1966 by Alfred A. Knopf, Inc

Chapter 4 originally appeared in *Nature* magazine and several of the drawings originally appeared in *The Living Wilderness* (now known as *Wilderness*).

Colorado Associated University Press is a cooperative publishing enterprise supported in part by Adams State College, Colorado State University, Fort Lewis College, Mesa College, Metropolitan State College, University of Colorado, University of Northern Colorado, University of Southern Colorado, and Western State College.

The reprint of this book was made possible by a generous gift from Jennifer and Edmund A. Stanley, Jr.

To the people of JACKSON HOLE

The wonder of the world, the beauty and
the power, the shapes of things, their
colours, lights, and shades; these I saw.
Look ye also while life lasts.

From a plaque over the mantel at Moose.

*Originally from an old gravestone in
Cumberland, England.*

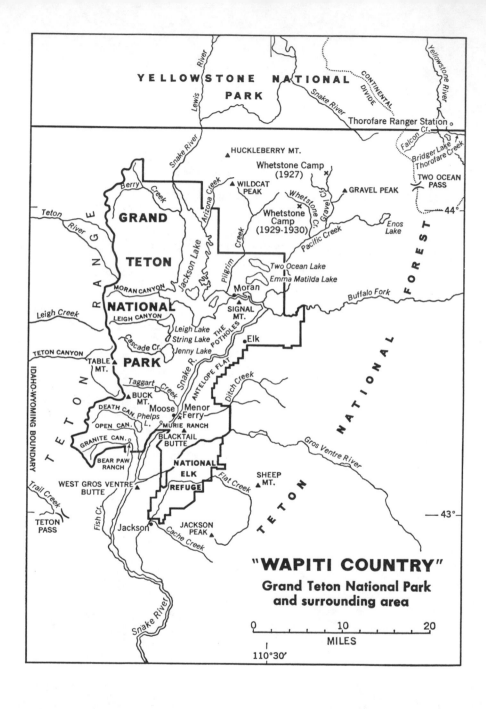

"WAPITI COUNTRY"

Grand Teton National Park
and surrounding area

Foreword

This beautiful part of America, the Jackson Hole country, was our home and the locale of much of Olaus's professional work for the past thirty-six years. Our three children grew up here, and while Olaus's work took us to many wilderness areas, this particular one has been our home. Naturally, over the years, we gathered many stories about this valley and about the people who lived and worked here. In working and thinking over these materials, it seemed to us that there were some stories he should tell and some that I should tell. So we wrote this book as a joint enterprise and tried to weave the narratives and the impressions together into a harmonious whole. Some of Olaus's contributions to the book were completed by him just before his last illness, but many of the chapters here, both his and mine, grew over the years, accumulated informally in our files for the time when we would write just such a book. Many people, biologists, ranchers, townspeople, guides, the wives of many of these, helped us learn about this country and, by their own lives and inspiration, contributed to this book. To all of these people, I wish to extend Olaus's and my own acknowledgment for that assistance. The quotation facing this page expresses what the

authors have felt about the wapiti wilderness. We had hoped
that this book might stimulate something of the same feeling
about all the natural world.

September 1965   Margaret Murie

Contents

WAPITI
WILDERNESS

The chapters written by Margaret Murie bear the

symbol ⟨ *M·M* ⟩

and those written by Olaus Murie the symbol ⟨⟨ **O·M** ⟩⟩

Introduction

Many times we have crossed Wyoming on the Union Pacific Railroad, usually in early or late winter. Riding in the dome car, I have watched fellow passengers, their eyes glazed with boredom, and I have listened to them:

"We should have given all this back to the Indians."

"Well, this is sure a God-forsaken piece of country, isn't it?"

"How would you like to live here? What do you suppose they can raise here? What's it good for?"

Good for? To one who has lived nearly always in the emptier places, to one returning to them after a few months in cities, it is a different picture:

At last, the wide sky, the wide land, broken and bare but stretching far to the limitless blue sky of Wyoming. Room to breathe, to stretch one's soul's wings again. Here the big country still is. Always a joy to come back, to find it still big, still stretching away, meeting and passing startling buttes which rise here and there, and dry watercourses, drift fences, once in a while a ranch house and corrals nestling under cottonwoods and willows in one of those watercourses; once in a while a few cattle, a band of antelope in the sage, some horses galloping with the wind.

After the cities, a wave of thankfulness rises in my heart, that the great United States still has some room, some great spaces. And sometimes there is a temptation to rise up in that dome car on the railroad and deliver a little lecture on what we are looking at here. I would like to read to these bored passengers a little essay I had found tucked away in some of Olaus's notes:

"I have had many opportunities to enjoy the beauties of Wyoming's sagelands. This was one of them. Mildred and Mardy and I drove south into the desert, the sage plains, to a watering place, a little pond in the desert. An old-timer had given Mildred a sketch map to guide us, and we had driven for several miles on a faint track. We wanted to photograph antelope, and anything else we could find. We made camp simply, laying out our sleeping bags, setting up a little photographic blind of green canvas near the waterhole; and cooking some steaks over a fragrant fire of dead sagebrush while we watched the sunset in a world of absolute stillness.

"After dark, I lay there in my sleeping bag, listening to a coyote howl, faint and faraway, and thinking about what is taking place on our big land and in our culture. Here at this waterhole sheepherders had been with their flocks. At the same time, there were we, eagerly looking forward to the morning, when we hoped antelope and other wild things would come in to drink at this little pond in the sagelands. Later in the season, hunters would be roaming over these plains. All of us, those concerned with raising livestock, those of us interested in pictures of wildlife and wild flowers, and the sportsmen, all find something in this environment, according to our needs and desires. This, I thought, is a sample of cooperation, of diversity, of democracy—so much on trial today, and all possible here in the open land.

"In the gray dawn Mildred and I were crouched in the blind, and the waiting was not long. Over a slight rise in the distance came seven horses, trotting unconcernedly to the water, drinking their fill, then suddenly galloping off through the sage, wild and free. As the light grew stronger, the sky bluer, a band of fifteen antelope came stepping down more cautiously, drinking daintily, tawny and white shadows reflected in blue water.

"Mildred's movie camera was whirring beside me; my still camera was clicking. Then she nudged me and whispered: 'Look over there, under the sage.' Here they came, gray shadows sliding out from gray sage, a covey of sage grouse, drinking and melting away again into the desert, unalarmed.

"We had had a glimpse of the real life of a bit of unaltered West, we hoped we had recorded it on film, and we felt enriched."

This is the wide desert scene of Wyoming. But the land rises and climbs as you go westward, and there is another world, a mountain world of very special and extraordinary beauty. Somehow the wide free sageland, the spacious desert and all its creatures, seems a fitting introduction to the mountains, a contrast yet a harmony, for it is all the natural free earth. Man is here, but he has not yet laid a heavy hand on his surroundings.

I

Into the Home of the Wapiti

{{ O·M }}

In June 1927 I was in Washington, D.C., to confer with my superiors in the United States Bureau of Biological Survey. After six years of work on natural history in Alaska, a new chapter was opening for me and my family. Here was something new and exciting, a challenging adventure. I was to make a complete study of the life history of the famous elk herd of Jackson Hole, Wyoming.

The elk herd, estimated at about 20,000 animals, the largest herd in the world, seemed to have fallen on evil times. Jackson Hole people, and state and federal officials, were much concerned. There had been a great deal of newspaper and magazine publicity about "the starving elk of Jackson Hole." The Izaak Walton League of America, the American Nature Association, the American Forestry Association, were all raising money with which to purchase private lands to be added to the already established National Elk Refuge adjoining the town of Jackson at the south end of the valley of Jackson Hole just south of Yellowstone, so that there would be more winter forage for the elk when they came down from the hills in winter. Finally the President had appointed a national "Elk Commission" to correlate the existing information and to make recommendations. One of the recommendations was that the Bureau of Biological Survey assign a research biologist to a thorough study of the life history of the elk and every factor affecting their welfare, this study to take whatever length of time was needed to make it complete.

This was just the kind of free yet demanding assignment I loved. The people in the Washington office gave me every bit of information and help they could, and I had long talks with the Chief, Dr. E. W. Nelson, and with the Chairman of the Elk Commission, the famous sportsman-naturalist Charles Sheldon.

Mardy was across the country in Washington State with her parents, with our two-year-old Martin and his very new sister Joanne, whom I had not yet seen. I headed west on the first of July, traveling by train to the north entrance of Yellowstone National Park.

As I entered the Yellowstone I was overwhelmed by a feeling that has lingered through the years and is hard to put into words. As I crossed the boundary on that bright summer day, it seemed as if the country itself suddenly changed. I was entering a different world. I suppose in the back of my mind was the thought that here was a region dedicated away back in the other century—first and very importantly at a campfire of civilian explorers, and later by our Congress—the first national park on this planet. As I rode to Mammoth Hot Springs on the bus, the surrounding country seemed something special. That evening I wandered out from the hotel to the hot springs, the first fascinating exhibit in this world of earth wonders.

A different kind of exhibit which did not please me so deeply was a series of cages near the park headquarters, holding native animals of the region. I recalled too clearly my own boyhood escapades, including holding a red fox captive for a time in a too-small box, and could understand the mistaken ideas of the administrators of this national park, but I am glad that this sort of exhibit was soon done away with.

Mass recreation had not yet, in 1927, invaded Yellowstone. It was not crowded. The bus trip down through the park to the south entrance was a leisurely one. Never again can I have quite the same feelings in visiting a newer, modern national park. Yellowstone will always remain something unique.

At the same time, my thoughts were eagerly reaching south toward that valley of the wapiti, the elk. On still another bus, late in the day, I arrived at the village of Moran and in the dusk, across Jackson Lake, saw those peaks rising straight up on its western shore, so startling I felt I was perhaps dreaming. This brief glimpse was all I saw of Jackson Hole until next day, for darkness was upon us, so that I first "saw" the valley by not seeing it.

There at the little log post office I met the mail carrier,

Charlie Hedrick, a bearded jovial woodsman. Later, when Charlie had become one of my good friends and a companion on several wilderness trips, I learned that the beard was worn to conceal scars of a boyhood encounter with a black bear. On this Fourth of July trip from Moran to Jackson there were troubles too—rough roads, streams to cross, frequent stops to pick up packages, messages—but Charlie took it all serenely. At one of the ranches along the route we picked up another passenger, a man who had broken his leg. We made him as comfortable as we could on the back seat of the old Ford and went rattling and bumping along through the dark. It seemed a long 34 miles.

As we neared the Gros Ventre River, Charlie told me the dramatic story of the great flood which had swept down upon them only six weeks earlier. Two years before, a great section of Sheep Mountain up the Gros Ventre River on the east side of Jackson Hole had suddenly slid into the valley, dammed the river, and formed a lake, moving earth, rocks, and forests clear up on the other side of the valley. This spring, without warning, the lake had broken through the dam and moved in a wall of water down the valley, carrying with it some of the little town of Kelly and several ranches and drowning several people. The bridge was gone, of course, but in the pitch dark Charlie found the ford and we splashed across and rattled on in to the town of Jackson and pulled up outside a neat white frame hotel, the Crabtree.

It was past midnight, the town had apparently finished its celebrations, and certainly we were not thinking of fire-

crackers! Charlie and I went into the lobby and he went through the hall and hammered on a door. "Hey, Henry, I've got two fellows here. One's O.K., but the other has a broken leg—you'll have to get Doc to look at him first thing in the morning, will you?"

I heard a sleepy but pleasant voice: "Put one in Number 7 and the other in 9—you know where they are, Charlie. I'll see to 'em in the morning first thing."

Thus I arrived in Jackson Hole.

The next thing I knew someone was pounding on my door: "Hey, Mr. Murie, you'd better come have some breakfast. I called Almer Nelson and he'll be in pretty soon."

The Crabtrees were taking care of me already! Rose and Henry they were, gray-haired handsome people. Her blue eyes sparkled with humor, and that she was a genius in the kitchen I saw right away. As we finished a bountiful breakfast in the big sunny room at the back of the hotel, a tall well-built blond young man with a smiling open countenance appeared in the door. "Hi, Almer," said Rose, "I know Loletta gave you a big breakfast about six o'clock, but come have a cup of coffee. Here's Mr. Murie who's going to help you find out all about those elk!"

Almer Nelson and I had one thing in common from the first—we were both Scandinavian, he of Danish parents and I of Norwegian. His eagerness to help, his great kindness, were evident from the first moment. By nightfall I had been taken out to Refuge headquarters a mile and a half from town, had met his auburn-haired wife Loletta, just as eager and just as kind as he, and their dark-haired year-old daughter Alma Ruth, who made me think all the more impatiently about the two-year-old and his sister; we had looked at the log house that the Crabtrees owned at the south edge of town—I had rented it and the Crabtrees and Almer had helped me move a few more pieces of furniture into it. Almer had even promised to help me build a baby crib before Mardy's arrival!

Besides all this, I had met the town. Jackson, unlike most western towns, and more like a New England village, is built around a Town Square, and Almer had taken me all around it, having me meet the proprietors of all the stores and the people at the bank, and the post office. I felt carried along on a wave of kindness, and jubilant that I could write Mardy that night and tell her to come as soon as she could, that I had found a home for us and that it would be among friendly people.

In the next few days Almer showed me all over the Elk

Refuge—the fields where the first hay crop was being harvested and stored to feed the elk when winter came; the additional lands which had been bought by the Izaak Walton League and the other organizations. I recalled that two years before Mardy and I had sent in five dollars, what seemed a large sum to us, not dreaming we would ever have any personal experience with those animals.

There were no elk in sight; they were far back in the hills to the north and east. But I began to get a picture of the scene of our next few years' living: the flat valley, the lower hills about the town, the broader valley and higher mountains north and east, the amazing Tetons on the west. There about the town and the Refuge were the buttes, with bare south slopes grass-covered at this season and dotted with bright flowers, wooded north slopes where the snow and moisture lingered longer into the spring. Over it all shone the bright sun, the sky seemed even bluer than in Alaska, the air at this 6,300-feet altitude was so stimulating I felt like starting right off afoot to find those elk.

As we were bouncing along over one of the back roads of the Refuge one day, Almer started chuckling: "You know, I might as well tell you—I have to laugh when I think of it, but when they wrote to me from Washington that they were sending a scientist out here to study the elk and I was to do all I could to help, I thought of course it would be some at least middle-aged fellow, probably with a beard! I was sure dumbfounded when I walked into the Crabtrees' kitchen that morning and saw *you!*"

2

"Getting to Know Them"

M·M

July 1927. By eight different conveyances Mother and I and
the two babies had made our way from Twisp, Washington,
to Jackson, Wyoming: by bus from the family home at Twisp,
by narrow-gauge railway from the little town of Pateros to
Wenatchee, by another train to Spokane and the welcome haven
of a Pullman car and berths; one day's travel with two-year-old
Martin and his seven-week-old sister Joanne. Next morning
we were in Butte, Montana, and spent seven hours in a hotel
room, where Martin amused himself by throwing his new
blue cap out of the window onto the sidewalk below; at 6 p.m.
we boarded an antique car on the Oregon Short Line of the
Union Pacific Railroad, with seats of red plush and iron filigree.
At 1 a.m. we arrived in Idaho Falls. The kindly brakeman
turned us over to the policeman standing on the platform, who
bundled us and the luggage and the sleeping babies into his

car and took us to a hotel, where we literally collapsed and slept a deep sleep until wakened at 7 a.m. by a fire engine going by. "Wait till I tell Olaus his family were in the hands of the police!" said Mother.

The sixth conveyance brought us by snorts and jerks and whistle blowing, and stops at every little farm town in that part of Idaho, to Victor, the end of the line at last, at two o'clock in the afternoon. There followed the hair-raising and unspeakably beautiful ride in a hired car up over Teton Pass and down the sixteen switchbacks through a fairyland of blossoms into Jackson Hole and on to the town of Jackson, six o'clock of a warm sunny July evening.

I hardly saw the town, only vaguely thinking it looked just like a movie set for a Western, there on the flat valley floor with bare buttes and a wooded one rising around it. My one thought was Olaus, would he be there, and what would he say about his daughter, whom I thought the most beautiful baby in the United States of America at that moment? The car passed through the main part of the town and pulled up beside a large log cabin on the sage-covered flat.

"I reckon this ought to be the one," said the kindly driver, and there was Olaus hurrying across the porch. Mother got out of the car, holding Joanne in her arms. "I don't know whether I'm going to let you see this or not," she said to Olaus, but held the bundle out to him. "My gosh—oh, gee whiz, isn't she wonderful?" And then he gathered me and Martin both into his arms too. We were together again, after four months.

The big log cabin with its roomy living room and red

brick fireplace looked like heaven to me. I had thought we might be living in a tar-paper shack, and didn't care; but this was extra good fortune—four big rooms.

A week later Almer Nelson, eager helper in every phase of this study of the elk, was taking us and the babies and our gear, and Mother, up the Pacific Creek road into the elk summer range and our first camping in Jackson Hole. Olaus could lose no time in getting out into the hills with the elk.

In those days the Pacific Creek road in Teton National Forest, toward the northeast "corner" of Jackson Hole, was little more than a track, up hill, down dale, over little streams, through boggy places, around lovely little ponds, through meadows of gay mountain flowers, through stretches of thick spruce, fir, and aspen. The Model T Ford bounced and churned merrily along; Joanne slept in my arms most of the way, and Martin, on Mother's lap, gazed steadily at everything along the way as though trying to understand all this new world. At the end of the road, eleven miles from the highway, we found the packhorses and the cooperative Forest Ranger, and fifteen-year-old Billy, son of Charles Sheldon, chairman of the Elk Commission. He had come to spend the summer with Almer and Loletta Nelson, and with us, and now he was to be Olaus's "field assistant."

Four hours of walking later, Olaus and Billy and the babies, and the horses, and I were alone in the Teton wilderness, the summer home of the elk, the wapiti. I stood and looked back through the forest, down the trail along which Mother and Almer had disappeared a few moments earlier, and reminded myself: "You're a grown woman now, remember; you can't always have your mother around to help you."

I hoped they would get back to the Model T before dusk, and that they would not have too much trouble getting up that peculiar little hill, so steep it looked impossible, that they would reach the highway before dark. But now, to make a home here. There were a few mosquitoes humming about. Martin was sitting on a rolled-up sleeping bag, looking bewildered, rubbing mosquitoes off his face. (Weeks later Almer told me: "You know, all the way back down the trail, I kept thinking of Martin; what a good little kid he was, sitting there just swatting mosquitoes and not saying a word!")

So first some mosquito ointment on Martin, and some on the baby in the tent, and a cookie from the lunch bag for Martin. Olaus was fixing sleeping places and the beds in the big tent; Billy was pitching his Boy Scout tent a few yards away. The tents were on a bench above the huge far-stretching Pacific Creek Meadows. Behind us rose hills clothed in forest, pine, spruce, and fir; before us, the meadow with the big creek wandering through it, and lower forested hills beyond. A gentle, encouraging scene; and soon there was a little fireplace of stones and the grate over it, and a pot of mulligan made of canned soup, and macaroni simmering in it. It was nearly dark, getting cooler, and that I learned right then is one of the blessings of Jackson Hole; the nights are cold enough so that the mosquitoes usually disappear. After all the years in Alaska, the Jackson Hole mosquitoes have always seemed hardly present to Olaus and me, anyway.

Martin made no protest that night at being fed quickly

and put into his Dr. Denton sleepers and tucked by his daddy into his down sleeping bag; it had been a big day for a two-year-old—for us all. The baby had been nursed and washed and tucked in also, while Billy, quiet, brown-eyed Billy, willing and skillful, had kept the fire going under the dinner. All was quiet and there was complete peace as we three finally sat down on a log near the fire, plates in laps—mulligan, fresh bread and jam, tea for Billy and me. And as we crawled gratefully into our sleeping bags, a great horned owl spoke from up the hill behind us—like a friend from Alaska welcoming us to Jackson Hole.

Billy was only fifteen, but had been trained well in woodcraft by his famous outdoorsman father. He was a willing and capable helper about camp, an eager follower of Olaus into the hills—looking for elk, observing them, and full of intelligent questions. More important to me, he was fond of the children, patient with Martin, taking him on little expeditions about the meadow and into the woods. As I worked about the camp I would hear their conversations: "See that bird up there Martin? That's a Clark's nutcracker. Can you say 'Clark's nutcracker'?"

"Cah-h—nuh-cah-r."

"Try again—Clark's nutcracker."

"Cah nuh-cah-r."

One morning as I sat in the tent nursing Joanne, Martin burst in: "Look, Mommy, look—nake, Mommy, nake!"

He held out to me a wriggling garter snake about six inches long. Here was a test! Olaus would be most disapproving if I ever indicated to our children that any form of life was ob-

noxious. I gulped once and said: "Oh, it's *lovely*! Take it quick and show it to Daddy!"

On the third day, with camp and its routine pretty well established, Olaus and Billy were gone into the hills for the day when this smiling, gentle Jackson Hole country gave me the first untoward experience. I had been raised in Alaska—hardly knew what a cow looked like—and when I stepped out of the tent that afternoon after putting Martin down for his nap, and found eighty head of white-faced Hereford range cattle gathered just in front of the bench, all looking up at the tent, I nearly collapsed! If they had been grizzly bears I would have felt much more at ease. Here were creatures I knew nothing about. If they stayed down there on the meadow, fine—but if they should decide to come on up, all of them, and investigate this strange new thing in their environment—what then? Could I climb a tree with a baby on each arm?

When the men returned that evening the white-faces were still there, feeding near the foot of the little bench, looking up frequently at camp, and the biologist's wife was in anything but a calm or optimistic frame of mind.

"They aren't supposed to be up this far," said Olaus calmly. "Come on, Billy, we'll chase them back down to the mouth of Whetstone."

They got back on their horses and trotted down onto the meadow, yipping as they thought cowboys should. The cattle went before them, and after a while the cowboys came back, well pleased with themselves, and picketed the horses for the night. I calmed down and got dinner ready, but just as I was about to call the family to eat I heard a sound across the little gully just south of camp. From behind a spruce tree near the trail a white-face stared at me; from behind another tree, another. They had chosen the trail, this time! To horse, again! But I was relieved to hear Olaus say, when they got back that time: "I think we'll move, up to the head of Gravel Creek. I can't study elk in a country that's all tracked up with cattle. Their tracks are too much alike."

So we would be moving, but first Olaus wanted one day up at the head of Whetstone Creek, and he and Billy set off on their horses early in the morning.

I kept busy, and Martin was busy, too, playing in a sandbank nearby, and the cows did not come. There were big cumulus clouds in the west; we might have a thunderstorm, but I enjoyed thunderstorms and the Forest Service tent was new and tight. As I tucked Martin into his bed for his nap and changed the baby and put her down to sleep too, I heard a moaning outside. I stepped out through the front flaps of the tent, the moaning suddenly increased to a roar, and the whole tent collapsed behind me.

I pictured the two stout spruce poles, the "scissors" from the ridgepole, lying across each of the two children, but then Martin howled and I knew he was at least alive. But no sound from the baby, while I tugged frantically at the tent pegs at the back of the tent where the childrens' beds were; there was no chance of getting in quickly through the mass of canvas at the front. After what seemed an eternity of tugging, and praying aloud, and calling to Martin: "Mommy's coming, it's all right, just a minute," I wiggled under the canvas. One pole lay across the foot of Martin's sleeping bag, but not on him; he was howling with fright. I turned to the other side. Joanne lay there quietly blinking up at the canvas close to her face; the pole was about six inches from her head; she smiled contentedly as I lifted her!

Now it didn't matter at all that the storm was roaring outside; my whole self was one great thankfulness. But quickly to get the babies out of there and into Billy's pup tent, which stood firm and untouched. Then to crawl in again and get diapers, sweaters, blankets, some toys for Martin, so we could spend the rest of the day in that little tent. I glanced at the big black clouds and knew the rain was close, snatched the day's laundry off the nearby willows, threw a tarp over the wood supply and our outdoor kitchen and quickly crawled in with the children. And the rain came. But I learned this day that the black moods of Jackson Hole were never to last long— it rained and it hailed and the wind roared in the trees, and I huddled close to the children and told Martin stories, and in an hour it was all over. There was beautiful benign smiling Jackson Hole again, and in no time, in this climate, everything would be dry and life would be serene and sunny.

A rather strange-looking caravan I suppose we were, moving up to Gravel Creek. Billy went ahead, walking and leading his pinto pony, packed, and the three other horses, all packed, trailing behind. Then came Olaus with a packsack on his back. In the packsack sat Martin; in Olaus's arms a precious bundle, Joanne in her sleeping bag. Finally came Mardy carrying the good old Boston bag of baby needs.

Not far above our old camp, Gravel Creek ran into Pacific. "You shouldn't wade in this ice-cold water," said Olaus. "You know—you're nursing the baby."

He waded across, laid the baby bundle on a grassy spot under a willow, knelt down, took off the packsack, lifted Martin out, waded across the creek, took me on his back, waded across again. This performance we repeated four times as we followed the trail up Gravel Creek, climbing, winding through thick forest of pine, spruce, and fir, crossing little meadows ablaze with flowers. When we came out of the forest in mid-afternoon and looked down into a great circular meadow, Billy was there ahead of us, unpacking the horses, trying to decipher the many knots with which Olaus had tied those loads on. He had forgotten to have Almer show him the diamond hitch before he left us there on Pacific Creek. Almer was going to have a good laugh when he met us again at the road-end a few weeks hence.

Our new camp was a delight, and without white-faces peering at us. A promontory of open woodland rose above the meadow; Gravel Creek, winding through, flowed at its foot. Up here among the trees we made our camp. In the midst of the trees was a natural grassy opening and some convenient down logs; here we had our fireplace, and Olaus built a clever kitchen-table–cupboard affair from poles, which made all the difference in the camp work for me. Here was my little world for the rest of the summer while the men roamed near or far studying elk—the tents, the campfire, the cupboard, the logs to sit on, the creek at the front of the slope, where baby washing was rinsed and hung on bushes to dry; and sometimes a band of elk, feeding along across the meadow, warm brown against the green forest.

Martin was content with a few toys, a few picture books, sticks and stones, an old tin spoon and a sandbank to dig in. The baby ate and slept and grew. And typical Jackson Hole summer weather spread its serenity over all of life with blue skies, white clouds, hot sunshine. Now and then there would be another short storm; then we all snuggled into the big tent while I read aloud a book about Viking days called *The Thrall of Leif the Lucky*.

Billy often rode over to Gravel Lake, a mile or two away

from camp, and always came back with two or three nice cut-throat trout to cheer the menu. One very hot afternoon the children and I were all in the tent, which was pitched in the shade of a big spruce and kept fairly cool. I heard Billy come back, then heard his call: "Mrs. Murie, there are some people coming!"

I rushed out. Far across the meadow, a straggling line of weary-looking souls, three men and a young boy. I called to Olaus, he came and looked. "My gosh, I bet that's Dr. Hall, but why are they *walking*?"

It *was* Dr. Maurice Hall, parasitologist from the Bureau of Animal Industry, accompanied by two veterinary doctors from Montana, one with his thirteen-year-old son, and when we had welcomed them and they had collapsed in the shade and been given some cool drink, we learned that somehow they had missed all the instructions and arrangements which Olaus had left at Moran for them, missed the horses they were to have hired at a ranch, the sleeping bags, the food. Worst of all they had thought it wasn't very far to our camp, had started walking from the end of the road. Fifteen miles they had walked, an endless journey on a hot day for people not used to such exertion or such altitude. So here we were with four "house guests" without food or bedding; but they were charming guests and somehow we made out, as one always does. When they had toiled up that last little slope to camp and been met by a sturdy-two-year-old with curly yellow hair running to meet them, they had been amazed: "How did you ever get him up here?"

Olaus and I just looked at each other and smiled. A few minutes later there came a baby's wail from the tent. Dr. Hall looked at me, wide-eyed: "Don't tell me you have a *baby* here, too!"

Dr. Hall had come to show Olaus how to do a postmortem for parasites, an important thing in the elk study, so there was a day to collect an elk, a day to study it and show Olaus all the techniques, a day to rest in camp. But on the fourth day they must leave—not only was their time running out, but they were all three out of tobacco, Dr. Hall, Dr. Morrow, Dr. Baldwin. Early that morning I heard their voices: "Have you got your pipe?"

"Yes, and I've got my habit too—you got any crumbs of tobacco left?"

Dr. Hall had marveled at Martin's capacity for mush. Sitting on a log, with a block of wood in front for table, Martin quietly consumed any kind of mush, his silence only broken by the words "More mush," as he handed the empty dish to me. When Dr. Hall said goodbye, he came and took Martin into his arms, tousled the curly golden hair: "Goodbye, Mush-eater; you'll grow up to be a mountain man-biologist like your father."

Three weeks later, on our third wedding anniversary, Olaus and I were again on the Gravel Creek trail, going downhill this time, Billy with the horses ahead of us, Joanne in her daddy's arms, Martin trundling behind part of the time and part of the time falling sound asleep in the packsack on Olaus's back, head nodding with Olaus's pace, and the warm sunny skies of Jackson Hole over our heads, the scent of pine and spruce in the little summer breeze making us even more aware of health and well-being. At the first crossing of the creek Olaus turned to smile at me: "It's been good, hasn't it?"

Already we were looking forward to another spring and more living in the mountains with the elk.

3

Spring in Jackson Hole

{{ O·M }}

I had stopped to rest on a boulder on top of a low butte at the north end of the Elk Refuge. It was one of those fresh-cool days of early spring when you just must walk out among the aspen trees, looking for things—anything that confirms what you already know. The blue mountains are inviting, you like to clamber among the cliffs. The previous night's frost has disappeared as the sun has risen higher. It is the time of running water, trickling off the slopes, singing down the watercourses. Windflowers have been reported already and the aspen grove on Kelly Hill behind the town has that pale tender green, the hue of awakening verdure that the whole town awaits. At this time of year people greet each other on the street: "I think I can see a little green on the hill."

The day before, a Sunday, the whole family had gone out to the Elk Refuge and climbed the little butte. The day was surprisingly warm, water running in a heavy stream out of the gap in the butte. We crossed it by walking on the rails of the experimental corral. Bare ground again on the slope of the butte, a bluebird or two, a pair of magpies, a killdeer at the spring. Up on the butte among the scattered dwarf cedars we watched a band of twelve deer. And as we came back down, there were three redtail hawks swooping and swinging high in the air, feeling the exuberance of spring. The warm south wind was in our faces and the children raced down the slope, wanting to fly too.

Not all of winter was gone. Behind me as I sat on that rock a company of tall willows stood waist deep in a lingering snowdrift. But they had felt the tickle at their toes; their buds were swelling and their catkins were out. Yet already I am afraid the spring will pass too fast. I want to reach out and hold it. I want it to stop and stay awhile, this promise, this eagerness, to hold off the fulfillment for a while. I want the thrill of stepping on the first bare ground, to feel the first release from winter cold. A week ago it was thirty below— today the water is running everywhere and the air is balmy. This sudden rush of spring birds, bluebirds, juncos, noisy killdeers, soaring hawks, has brought a sudden aliveness to the land. The falcon is back on the butte, passing and swooping over the old nest site on the cliff.

My thoughts as I sat there on that big rock went back to the exuberant days of the Indian and the mountain men. John Colter was here, in 1807. Osborne Russell, a century ago, had looked upon this scene. The Gros Ventre Indians had passed through here. They had all viewed this valley at the foot of the Teton Mountains, had seen those distant blue hills in the north where the game herds summer. They knew that line of cottonwoods where Snake River moves down in front of the high range. They had seen antelope and bison wandering freely over these sagelands and meadows of the middle of the valley.

Overhead I heard the swish of wings. Five ravens, soaring, diving, playing in the air, with gurgling notes of ecstasy. Close to me a bluebird flitted in over the gray slope and perched in a sage bush—the bluebird, eagerly looked for by present-day schoolchildren, who have built birdhouses for it. In those other days it had fluttered among Indian tepees, and the clowning ravens had been a familiar sight to those early Westerners.

I was so engrossed for the moment with those robust days of long ago that I was only dimly aware of a movement at my left. Then I suddenly realized there were gray shadows moving among the aspens, then a line of elk stringing out into the open. So thoroughly did they fit into my dream of yesterday that it took me several moments to come back to the present.

I watched them leave the shelter of trees and strike out across the open sage—northward. This, too, was a part of spring in Jackson Hole. Their winter coat was coming loose, in ragged shreds, leaving dark bare patches of skin. A tattered moth-eaten lot of creatures, but underneath the winter-worn exterior burned an age-old urge and as they moved away into better perspective the scars of winter were lost to view and the elk were transformed before my eyes into shapely wild animals in graceful silhouette, with twinkling feet. As they moved out in front of the line of stark and bare cottonwoods with the Tetons beyond, the beauty and significance of it was breathtaking.

For how many centuries, how many springs, had this been going on? Little bands of elk, one by one, venturing out across the floor of Jackson Hole; bands of them moving across the foothills over on the east border of the valley; old bulls with shaggy necks, and velvet knobs already swelling on their antler pedicels; cows shedding their hair and heavy with calf; yearlings, two-year-olds; the elk tribe, the wapiti tribe, the survivors of winter, moving north. Spring migration!

Can you remember, when you were a child, if you lived in snow country, the eager zest with which you planted your feet on the first patch of bare ground? Was it not a kindred exuberance that caused the elk to hop in crazy capers and toss their heads on those first mild days of early spring? I think we can feel with them, experience with them if we will, the primal instincts and the early stirring of aesthetic satisfactions, simple and crude perhaps, but true and unmistakable. I looked north to the far low hills at the north end of the valley and visioned their routes of travel—to such places as Pilgrim Creek, Two Ocean Lake, Pacific Creek, and even beyond to the upper Yellowstone.

It is exhilarating to think that the surge of life on our planet is older than the earth features we now can see. Men of science with a geologist's hammer and notebook, a keen eye, strong limbs, and deep understanding of the behavior of the earth's crust have climbed and dug and tapped among our mountains. They have found fossils on mountain tops, declaring these were at one time the bottom of an ocean. They have been over the Rocky Mountains. They have been in the Teton Range. The story they tell is tremendous. They speak of the torsions and bending and buckling of the earth's crust as we would speak of the cracking open of a cake in the oven. They tell us of the turmoil at the earth's surface that broke out in what we know as the Rocky Mountains and the Andes, in a line from Alaska to Cape Horn, a good way round the globe.

One episode in this global upheaval was a cracking of the earth's crust and an upthrust in what is now western Wyoming. This fault block presented its perpendicular steep edge eastward some sixty million years ago, they tell us. Erosion, running streams, glaciers carved this eastern edge into what we know today as the Teton Mountains. Perhaps the mountain sculpture we see here today was largely accomplished in one of the interglacial periods of the great Ice Age—so recent that man himself could almost remember!

And the wapiti? This race of noble deer has its remnants far-flung over the earth's surface. In Mongolia, in northern China and Tibet are wapiti to this day with the carriage, the form and essential character of the herds of Jackson Hole. In the Pleistocene loess formations of interior Alaska the placer miner washes out the bones and antlers of wapiti—bones and antlers indistinguishable from those of modern animals. We speak of migrations to and from the mountains. Consider the global travels of animals—centuries of reaching out for new pastures, new lands inviting settlement. Here, there, and beyond were found suitable homelands throughout Eurasia. Who shall say where it all started? A branch of this deer group explored westward and populated Europe and parts of Asia—the local red deer of today. The wapiti branch seemed to have explored eastward. It was inevitable that they should discover the Bering Sea, some of which was dry land. Siberia and Alaska being then solidly connected, the wapiti found it simple in their wanderings to discover Alaska, as did the mountain sheep, the brown bear, and much later, across a narrow strait, the Indians and the Eskimo.

So these animals came to this continent and spread from the Pacific to the Atlantic, from parts of Canada to Mexico. They were never at home on the desert, but managed to find the alpine summits of desert mountains. Then in the north, that between-land of the Pleistocene was flooded and formed the shallow Bering Sea. Climate barriers closed in behind them. The wapiti, together with the wild horse and the mammoths, vanished from interior Alaska. We find only their bones today on the river bars. But the wapiti immigrants had found a home to their liking farther south.

We laud the exploits of human pioneers. We trace their travels over the lands of the earth, their voyages over the seas. They too found new homes to their liking. They were but following the tradition of earlier pioneers, the wapiti, the bighorn, the mammoth, the tiny songbirds, kindred all.

In his exuberance man proceeded to destroy previous pioneers—the bison, the wapiti, and the Indian. Under the thin veneer of sensitivity and intellectual awareness such as the world had never before witnessed, lurked still a savage nature that trampled all hindrances before it. The wapiti, the bison, the pronghorn were swept from the earth—almost. The wapiti found a refuge in a few wilderness retreats. The largest remnant clung to Yellowstone and Jackson Hole.

As today, then, we watch these winter-worn ragged creatures moving up the valley toward the promise of summer pastures, we may admire them in the picturesque country they inhabit, but more than that we may allow our minds to roam over the centuries, to view these animals in the perspective of earth-shaping forces, the perspective of animal history. These are the descendants of the pioneer hordes, emigrants from strange far lands. These are the early settlers of Jackson Hole.

One thing I could wish, and that is that there was not this confusion about their name. As I watched that band of spring migrants disappearing into a grove of cottonwoods north of the rocky knoll where I sat that spring day, I thought of my speech of a few days before, trying to explain all this to Mardy: "You see, they of course had no 'name' when they came here; when the Indians came much later and found them, they called them 'wapiti,' and as near as I have been able to find out 'wa' means light-colored; they must have looked lighter to them than some other animal they knew, maybe the bison. Now, the animal we call moose here, which is also an Indian word, also lives in Europe and is called in Germany 'elch' and in Norway 'elg,' and I guess when the first men came from Europe they began calling the wapiti 'elk'—perhaps before they ever saw a moose over here; and the animal in Europe which is closely related to the wapiti, so close that they will cross-breed, is called the red deer—that's the 'stag at eve.' It's not what we would call a deer over here at all. Do you see?"

"No, I can't say that I do," had been Mardy's reply. I couldn't blame her! And I suppose the wapiti will continue to be called elk in North America, while in far-away New Zealand the animals that have been introduced from Jackson Hole and Yellowstone are called by their correct North American Indian name, "wapiti"!

We cannot follow the elk in all its wanderings. We have become too dependent on a bed to sleep on, prepared food. And if the elk should run for a bit, to get somewhere in a hurry, we are left behind. But we can look on them now and then, catch them at their daily routine from time to time.

The little band I had seen burst out of the aspen grove and start out across the flats had a long way to go—at least 35 to 40 miles, perhaps 50 or more, before they would feel that they were back home for the summer. Across the sagelands they wandered, wavering a little uncertainly. At the Gros Ventre River they felt more comfortable, among the cottonwoods, but no place to linger there. Out in the open again, traveling parallel with the towering Teton Range a few miles to the west; but at the north end of the valley they struck timber again and felt more secure. From there on they traveled by devious ways, hidden from the sight of man, on to Two Ocean Lake, to Pacific Creek, or Pilgrim Creek. There they would linger a while.

. . .

"In the nice ear of Nature, which song was the best?"

What passes in the mind of a cow elk in the month of May? Is she conscious of the coming event? Certainly she must be aware of the new life she is nurturing within.

We are accustomed to think of the big bull doing all the bugling, especially in the fall of the year, when he makes music on the mountainsides. We think of the cow as silent and un-picturesque. But observe her closely in the month of May. Over there among the aspens an elk is bugling. Bugling in May? That should be in autumn, in the breeding season, shouldn't it? But if you carefully creep up on that sound you may find only a cow. Watch a while. Presently she extends her muzzle and bugles again. Not, to be sure, with quite the ringing performance of the big bull in the autumn, but bugling nevertheless. What is the reason for this? We think of bugling as a challenge. Perhaps we should revise our thought on this.

Then we recall that this is the culmination of the sexual cycle, the time when the instincts of motherhood are awakened. Is it not logical that the elk mother-to-be should give voice to some kind of parental emotion? And to us, watching quietly from the aspens, she is the female herald of spring, of birth and re-birth, and awakening.

Here in this aspen grove, awakening is all around us; the aspens are green, their light smooth trunks shining, and the forest floor thick with springing new green herbs. Jackson Hole would not be the same without the aspen. We admire the massive Douglas fir, the blue spruce of the river bottoms, the rugged scraggly spread of the white-bark pine at timber-line. But there is an especially warm spot in our hearts for the quaking aspens that rim our valley and clothe the foothills. Each season the aspen has its special charm. No need to com-pare other seasons with the golden glory of autumn, any more than one would contrast a brilliant sunset with the velvet soft-ness of the deep woods at dusk. In early spring when buds begin to burst, a flush of pale green spreads over the groves, faintly at first, barely distinct from the earlier gray, but deepen-ing day by day to a lively light green, vibrant above the gray sage and the deeper green grasses coming up.

Some of the finest aspen groves are in the region of Two Ocean and Emma Matilda Lakes, and that's the place for spring! The cow elk think so too, for this is one of their favorite calving grounds. There is a little stream which runs down a slope through the aspens, out across a green meadow and into the willows of a swamp. We had our camp just within the margin of the aspens, at the mouth of a little glen, against the foothills. Here we would spend the spring days; here for six years we started our summer season with the wapiti. Here I could easily make observations on behavior of cow elk, on the birth and infant life of the calves, until the whole band would move farther into the hills, up toward Pacific and Whetsone creeks, and we would follow along with them.

The spring Martin was nearly four he went with me on many searches for new baby elk—walking quietly through the sage, under the aspens on the grassy slopes above Two Ocean Lake, or across the flat meadows and around the marshy inlets back from the lake; and sometimes I would hear his urgent whisper: "Daddy, right there—behind that sage brush!" And we would walk together very slowly to gaze down upon a little spotted gold-and-white calf curled upon itself, nose close to the ground, motionless, but big eyes wet and bright. Quickly I would snap a picture, take Martin by the hand, and silently we would step back. And always there was the mother, anxiously watching from the edge of the woods.

Under the blue sky of spring we watched more than elk, for the spring world of Jackson Hole is one of endless enchantment. There were moose mothers and young too, and mule deer. Often we saw a black bear ambling up some slope through the aspens; one day as the children played outside our tent a brown cub came running right through camp beside the children, jumped the tiny creek, disappeared up the slope. Here was excitement to talk about all the rest of the summer.

But the children learned to know smaller companions too;

ground squirrels popping out of their holes to squeak at them; striped chipmunks sharing all their play places among down logs and bushes; a jumping mouse suddenly leaping before them through the grass. They learned to look up, too, to see hairy woodpeckers or sapsuckers feeding babies in a hole in an aspen, tree swallows darting over their heads, Clark's nutcrackers calling noisily from the tops of the pine trees. All this life was the background of their own life in spring camp.

Every spring we also hiked from camp through meadow and forest to Emma Matilda Lake. There was no road, hardly a trail, so it was quiet there and we found the quiet-loving birds. Always some trumpeter swans, and loons, very rare in this valley, and bitterns and herons and many kinds of ducks. Here too we searched for elk calves in the aspen groves.

Evenings were full of spring sounds too. After we had had supper by the campfire, Mardy and the children and I would walk down the dirt road toward Two Ocean Lake, often stopping in the dusk to see how many songs we could hear. The marsh running back from the lake was full of frog song, and even Joanne knew this was "froggie music," not bird song. But rising above this symphony, from the aspen groves and willow thickets, came the songs of the fox sparrow, the song sparrow, the Lincoln sparrow; from farther over in the depths of the woods, the serene notes of the hermit thrush.

When we returned in the last of dusk the nighthawks would be zooming over the meadow below camp, but the children had learned that this bird was not zooming at *them*. He was just a part of their spring world, making his living in his own way.

Sometimes a little incident, a brief experience, reveals so much of the character of an animal. I was coming out of heavy lodgepole forest. Ahead of me lay a series of rolling meadowlands and I quickly spied in the distance a large band of elk. I was surprised at their numbers, and hurried forward with the camera. Halfway there I stopped to count them with the aid of binoculars. There were 182, twenty-five of them calves. I paused a while to view the scene and recalled a page of instructions about taking photographs. You must include some interesting details in the foreground, or your composition won't be good. The real thing I feel must be different. Perhaps when you condense a landscape down into the confines of a small frame you must do those special things to hold the attention. But when the landscape itself rolls out before you a half mile, a mile, or more, reaches on around you, takes you in and makes you a part of it, you don't seem to need artistic props. I was only conscious of an expanse of green earth, rich green sod, heavy and sedgy over in the wet meadow, curving up smoothly on the nearby rise, to meet scattered patches of purple-gray sage. Near at hand I vaguely sensed the pale greenish-white anemone, the pink and white sprinkling of spring beauties, the still-folded buds of blue camas. But in the distance all the plants merged into a smooth wash of green sloping up to the inviting pine forest. And there, in the middle distance, a long restless string of elk gave life and action to the living picture. It was pleasing just to stand there and feel a part of the wide sweep of earth, to be just another creature on the face of Nature.

But presently I continued on, for a closer look at the elk.

A few alert cows raised questioning ears, gazed at me intently as I approached, then trotted off. But they had no great following. The herd was too big. Some were lying down, others milled around aimlessly.

I may have disturbed the animals somewhat, to cause all that restlessness. But they are peculiar beings, and like the rest of us, when they get into a large crowd they lose much of their individual judgment. They wandered about, without purpose; occasionally a small group would become panicky, run off for the woods, and in a short time gain considerable following. Soon elk were streaming steadily into the woods. But many were left behind; all did not go. And pretty soon here came the others back again pell-mell to join the herd. This was repeated several times. Then they would mill around uncertainly—no mind to make up, apparently, and they didn't know what came next. A few gave up the problem altogether and calmly lay down in the grass. Why worry? They didn't care anyway.

The calves ran hither and yon among the grown-ups, trying desperately to keep track of their mothers. And when one of those confusing stampedes took place, what a babel of anxious squealing while they searched for their mothers again! But I felt the whole thing was exciting, and fun for the youngsters. They had just completed that first immobile period in their lives when they spent most of their time lying around in hiding, patiently waiting for Mother to come back and let them nurse. Now their legs were stronger. When the mothers ran from danger, fancied or real, they could keep up. They were part of the herd, and felt the delicious pulsing of young life. Their mothers, too, felt the exhilaration of the green season. The lean white winter was forgotten now, as if it had never been. They had been on green feed since the snowdrifts had made way for the new tender greenery. They were sleek and rounded; the sun glistened on their curves as they moved, and they showed their high spirits. Two cows would begin to hop and skip heavily, with clumsy bovine tossing of their heads; in this late afternoon coolness of a summer day there was no doubt about their joy in being alive. In the midst of flight, during one of those mild stampedes, some of them would forget what they were running for and would hop in a zigzag fashion as the playful mood came uppermost. Gradually the herd moved toward the woods, and some cows found a pool of water. Into the water they splashed, like a bunch of lively kids with their pants rolled up, and as the spirit rose, they pawed the water and the spray flew.

I followed rather closely, forcing the elk into the forest. I kept track of them by the squealing of the calves. Slowly, quietly I drifted in among the trees, and then realized the elk were straight ahead some 75 to 100 yards. I caught glimpses of red-tawny bodies moving in the trees, the sun glinting on their sleek coats here and there. Occasionally I became aware of a pair of ears nearby and a serious elk face ludicrously intent on scrutinizing me. I would stand still and try to outlast the patience of the suspicious one, until she went on, uneasily. They went deeper into the pine woods, and I returned to the open meadows and made my way back to camp.

Spring had reached its climax; the wapiti were moving higher into the mountains. Time for us to move with them.

4

Voices of the Moonlight

⟨⟨ O·M ⟩⟩

In the fall of 1928 my brother Adolph was able to stay late enough to help me on an autumn field trip before going back to the University of Michigan.

We planned to make a big sweep through the whole summer range country of the wapiti, to make almost a circle—going in near the south entrance of Yellowstone Park, through the upper Yellowstone and Thorofare country, over Two Ocean Pass, back to the Pacific Creek and Whetstone Creek country in Teton National Forest and so back to Moran in the main valley of Jackson Hole.

It was a fine trip, for it held variety—sunny warm days, days of cold lashing rain and even snow; cold mornings in camp when pack ropes and saddle pads were stiff with frost and defied the patience of our fingers. It also involved the unpredictable nature of horses, cast shoes, tangled picket ropes;

always the wonder whether they would all be there in the morning; and throughout the trip, there was Old Socks.

I had at that time only the wonderful sorrel mare who was always perfection, and the little white mule who trotted at her heels wherever she went, and The Black. We felt we needed another pack animal, and as Leek's Camp at the head of Jackson Lake was convenient for a starting point, we rented a packhorse from Steve Leek, one of the grand old pioneers of the valley, who was also a poet and photographer. Steve said he could spare Old Socks for two weeks. He said little more, but Mrs. Leek in her friendly voluble manner told us what a wonderful animal Old Socks was, their best packhorse. We had been on our way only a couple of days when we decided that Mrs. Leek had probably not been out on a pack trip with Old Socks for many years; that he may have been their best packhorse twenty years before. Now he was very tired. He would go his own pace and no faster, and that pace left him plodding along far behind the party.

Something had to be done. Adolph, riding The Black, offered to take the halter rope. After a few hours his arms were almost pulled from their sockets by the drag of that rope. On the third morning out I said at breakfast: "I guess we'll have to try something else. Let's see if we can tie his rope to Lady's saddle horn; maybe she can keep him coming."

So as usual the mare saved the situation for us; it ended up with her practically dragging Old Socks all through the Upper Yellowstone and down Pacific Creek. It saved our arms, and it kept Old Socks and his load with the expedition, but I am sure that if Lady could have talked she would have described the injustice of life! Besides which, the mule resented this strange animal taking her place at Lady's heels, and kept trying to edge him away.

The main object of this trip was to study the fall movement of the wapiti from their summer range, and for this purpose we were glad enough to have a skiff of snow, it made study and counting of tracks so much easier. But we were also interested in their rutting habits, and were glad for some warm sunny days when we could locate a band of elk and with our glasses observe them for several hours at a time. The changeable nature of the weather really suited us, and the days were full. We were also taking pictures, and setting out a trap line for small mammals each night, as Ade had a permit to collect for the University of Michigan museum. Several times we stayed over in one camp for two days, to give the horses a rest and have a chance to climb the slopes, scout out bands of elk, and watch them. Each night there were specimens to put up, notes to write, drawings to complete. Somehow we also managed to cook and eat; and always there were those horses to watch and wonder about!

In our second week out we found ourselves picking our way down from Two Ocean Pass and the weather seemed to have settled into that dreamlike Indian-summer period of late September and October for which Jackson Hole is famous, and which to my mind defies all superlatives. Aside from the one little fact of looking forward to saying goodbye to Old

Socks, we were sad to think that the trail would in a few days lead us out of the hills.

The country here was new to us and we eagerly scanned each turn in the forest trail for an opening, a vantage point from which to view the wider landscape. As the afternoon wore on, the monotonous creak of saddles, the steady nodding and plodding of the pack animals lulled our senses to drowsiness. Then, unexpectedly, we came into a meadow. Through a fringe of trees we glimpsed a great valley below us, a vast, flat grassland with scattered clumps of willow. Through it wound a silver ribbon. That would be the Upper Yellowstone! Through that cleft in the hills, yes, that must be the Thorofare. And there we shall camp tonight.

We moved forward with quickened interest and soon were threading our way through the swampy bottomland of the Yellowstone. A cow moose lunged off through the willows. We passed a beaver house in a blind channel. High overhead an eagle soared. The wide sweep of the valley landscape, sheer cliffs and bold mountain slopes with heavy green forest, the tange of autumn all added to the rapture of the moment. Here was wilderness.

We camped on the Thorofare that night. We had found a grassy flat beside the stream for our horses, and our tent was set snugly just within the edge of the woods. Around the Thorofare valley rose the mountains, steeply. In these clear bright days and frosty nights of perfect autumn, the moon was coming bigger and brighter every night. We had first noticed it back on Wolverine Creek when it had hung pale against the afternoon sky. Tonight it was full.

It is not my purpose to attempt an enraptured recital of the charms of moonlight, the province of the poet and the lover. But Lady Moon will always color man's life and I would suggest a corner of the wilderness as her shrine.

We had been across the river and were returning to our camp when we saw it up the valley, bulging over the skyline, a rich orange at first, with tree silhouettes moving across its face in a steady procession as we walked. Later it hung, pure silver now, suspended clear above the trees and the rough contour of surrounding mountains, looking down into our little nook in the wilderness.

I remembered that before sunset the pinewoods had stood about us in deep green, with a splash of gold among the aspens. The meadow lay bathed in rich yellow hues of autumn grass and brown of the willows, from pale greenish yellow to deep russet, with overlying tints of gray. Truly a rich display.

Now, by the alchemy of moonlight, all was transformed into a soft duotone of black and silver. The tiny meadow lay silver bright, overlaid with a dark tracery of moon shadows from the pines. On the forest floor about our tent lay the same network of shadowy limbs and twigs, while in the deeper woods a few gleams penetrated in scattered flecks that silvered the underbrush. We scarcely broke the silence with speech.

"It bothers me," I ventured. "I cannot grasp it all. I want to do something with it, but don't know what. It is this tiny little ache, with all the beauty, that stirs me."

I felt stupid at my own trite words. Who has not already said as much? An old, old yearning, this. But the fervent assent of my companion proved this yearning to be ever fresh.

We walked on in silence across the silver meadow to our camp.

"Who-whoo, whoo, whoo," came a soft voice up the valley.

"Who-who-who—whoo, whoo," came a higher voice in quick response.

Horned owl! All that was needed to give voice to the moonlight. But another sound broke in on the owl duet: "Eeee-ee-ee-ah-h-h-eough!"

A clear bugle call, rising in a silvery crescendo, falling gracefully to end in a low grunt; the bugling of a bull elk. His ringing call went echoing in a confusion of rippling sound among the mountain walls. We pictured him there on the opposite slope, the antlered master of his little harem. His was the fulfillment of elkhood, a bull in his prime, in mating time! Was this his challenge to any possible rival, to the world? Possibly, but more, I believe, an expression of his exuberance, his song, perhaps a little defiance mingled with the ardor of his lovemaking. And was it not, perhaps, colored a little by the flood of moonlight?

The owls, I knew, had long since raised their family. Who will fathom the intricacies of owl nature?

But there were other voices.

"Aooooo-o-o-oo-o-o," a long clear call rolled up the valley, mingling with its echoes and trailing off into silence. A rival bull elk?

"Yeow! Yeh! Yeh! Yeowoooo-o-o-o-o" was the answer, and we knew these were the ululations of coyotes. Hard upon these two came still a third, far down the valley: "Yah! Yah! Ow-ow—ow-a-a-a-a-ooooooo." Then the first again, until the ringing chorus and its echoes filled our valley to its brim. First one and then another lowered his voice. There were a few quavering notes, the echoes died, then silence. Once more the silver meadow, with its moon shadows, and the low murmur of the river.

We wondered. Were those other creatures of the night responsive to the spell of the moon? Are we human creatures the only ones who thrill to a silvery night? True, the day before we had heard the coyotes sing out in the garish light of midday. Perhaps the tang of autumn had been their inspiration. I once had two pet coyotes who each night were set off on a wild duet by the curfew whistle; a mechanical stimulus, surely. Nevertheless, it seems logical that these fellow creatures share with us in some degree the appeal of Nature's moods. True, they do not philosophize about it. We, ourselves, are often moved unreasonably.

As we lay abed, with the tent wide open to the moon, we were content. These woodland voices had enriched the night, had revealed to us the vibrant life lying hidden within the cover of our moonlit valley. We drowsed at the faint sound of the river.

But once more our consciousness quickened, for a new note, a distant throbbing, came to our ears.

"Thump, thup, thup, thup, thrrrr-rrrrr."

Surely the drumming of a ruffed grouse! What was he doing, drumming in September? The moon again?

Faintly it came again and again, until it mingled with the murmur of the river and merged into our dreams.

5

Summer on Whetstone Creek

M·M

Through Almer and Loletta we came to know the American Legion folks, and in those days this organization was most active in projects for the betterment of the town. They were all great dancers. Dances were different then. The music was live, the musicians were interesting to watch; and everybody, young and old, came to dance. Teen-agers had not yet been declared a species and a cult apart, and we all one-stepped, two-stepped, fox-trotted and waltzed and polkaed together in the old Clubhouse—a two-story log and frame building on the east side of the Square. The dance hall was upstairs over the drugstore. One evening during a dance Olaus and I went downstairs for a soda. The thunder, the shaking and vibration from the dancing feet above were terrifying. But the building stood, and has stood, all the years.

Liquor was not allowed at Legion dances. No one with

many drinks in him could have kept up with the vigorous Jackson Hole style of dancing anyway.

It was at the Legion dances that we met Buster and Frances Estes, who had a dude ranch fifteen miles north but always managed to get to town for all the Legion doings even in winter, and who were sincerely interested in the work Olaus was doing.

When we moved on into the hills that spring of 1929, Buster and Frances stole a few days away from opening up their dude ranch down the valley so Buster could help Olaus tag any wapiti and moose calves we might find near our spring camp. We were expecting two seventeen-year-old lads from Washington, D.C., but they had not yet arrived.

Olaus and Buster had just come in, breathless and muddy from a slight tussle with a moose calf in the swampy area below camp, when Joanne, who at the age of two was already earning her later gang nickname of "Hawk-Eye," cried out: "Car! Car!" and pointed to a puff of dust coming toward us over the rough dirt track from the south.

Here were our two summer guests and helpers, Fletcher Henderson, son of the associate chief of the Bureau of Biological Survey, and David Griggs, son of the famous geology professor who had discovered Alaska's Valley of Ten Thousand Smokes. The boys had driven David's old Chevrolet from Washington in four and a half days, no small feat in 1929. They were tired, dusty, hungry, and exuberant. Exuberant and hungry they remained until they left us on the first of September. My life and thought for the balance of that summer centered in the necessity of trying to fill those two to satisfaction if not to repletion. True, I had had, the summer before on Arizona Creek, my fifteen-year-old brother Louis in camp, but he was only one, though just as hungry.

My memory of the summer is studded with such items as 17 pounds of peanut butter, rice pudding cooked over the camp-fire in a small-size dishpan, and the two boys tossing a coin to see who got the last remaining piece of cake with chocolate sauce on it, which was a very special treat, the cake being baked with watchful care in our Yukon stove in the tent.

But the memory is also bright with the unfailing good nature and willingness and curiosity of those boys, their real interest in the children, their whistling about camp and singing about the campfire, their eagerness to hear all of Olaus's stories about animals and adventure, and to help him in his work.

When we were ready to follow the wapiti farther into the mountains, Olaus's mother had joined us. After fifty years in the flatlands along the Red River of Minnesota she was as though transported back to her native Norway. This summer she was to find endless delight in the mountain meadows, the little streams, the flowers, and rocks, but between Norway and Wyoming there was one added delight—cowboys! In the week's interval down in Jackson while we were refitting for the rest of the summer, she had attended the annual rodeo put on by the American Legion Post, and had fallen head over heels in love with cowboys: cowboys racing, cowboys roping, cowboys just standing around in their distinctive costumes; but above all, cowboys riding bucking broncos! When the third bucking horse charged out of the chute she turned to me and said: "We can save the money some other way. This is worth it!"

Her life had been one of constant frugality, and the one-dollar admission fee had bothered her.

Now on this sunny morning at the end of the Pacific Creek road she was to see a display of bucking without cowboys. The summer before, when we had camped at the head of Arizona Creek, the little white mule, blind in one eye, had carried both children very capably and safely in her canvas panniers—Martin on one side, Joanne, then just past a year, on the other—whenever we moved camp or wanted to go on a whole day's trip out from camp with the whole family. This spring Olaus had a better idea. He would put his big Graflex camera outfit in one pannier, Joanne in the other, and Martin, now four, could ride on a pillow on top of the pack saddle and hang on to the cross-trees; thus we would easily transport the whole outfit the four miles from the road head to our new camp at the forks of Whetstone Creek.

Joanne was put in the pannier and tied in securely; the cameras loaded into the other, Martin was set up on the saddle. The two boys and Grandma were over at the cars, unloading the last few items; I was holding the mule's halter rope. We had three horses: the beautiful sorrel mare, Lady; The Black—never called anything but "The Black"; and Tony, a new bay horse. Olaus knew that the mule objected to any other animal touching her, though she was meekness itself with people, so when he saw Tony turn in his place so that he might touch her hind quarters he quickly moved toward Tony to tie him to a tree farther over. But in moving around the mule, he unthinkingly laid his hand on her hip. And she exploded into action! At the first jump Martin was thrown off and landed right under her belly. Olaus reached for him but missed the first time—just as in an agonizing dream where all your motions are without power—but the next grab reached and rescued Martin. Olaus fairly threw him out of danger's way and rushed to the mule's head to help me. I was hanging obstinately to the halter rope, though there was such friction from the mule's wild lunges that my palms were rather badly rope-burned; and at the same time I was seeing Joanne, hanging out of the pannier head down and being thrown like a rag doll at every lunge, while in the dim distance of my mind I heard the boys yelling, "Hang on, Mrs. Murie, hang on!" But they were both so transfixed with horror that neither of them moved to my assistance until it was all over. In a moment Olaus had the mule under control; as soon as she saw him at her head and realized she was not being pushed around by a horse she was immediately quiet. The whole little drama must have taken place in the space of four seconds; but to Olaus and to me it remained forever a searing memory.

It need not be said that our children never again rode the mule! Beyond that, Martin was so marked by the experience that all the rest of the summer, every time he saw the mule following the mare and coming in from the meadow toward camp he would race to me, crying, "Mool! Mool!" And I have wondered if this may not be the underlying conditioning which has made him less than interested in horses or riding ever since!

For that day, David and Fletcher took turns carrying Joanne when she tired of walking, and David even carried Martin on his back part of the four miles, and we all tramped along behind the three packed horses, and the mule, with thankfulness in our hearts. Olaus never again tried to combine babies and cameras on a pack animal, and I know that beneath his quiet mien as he and the boys finished packing the horses, he was shaken by that brief nightmare. As for his mother, she was, under this stress, talking volubly in her native tongue.

Just below the confluence of the two forks of Whetstone Creek there is a large meadow, perhaps a quarter of a mile wide, reaching back to the edge of the lodgepole pine and fir forest clothing the hillsides. In the edge of the forest, with the meadow before us, we set up our camp for the rest of the summer, and in only a few hours it was Home.

Just as one settles into the atmosphere of a house which is to be a home, its various rooms, hallways, windows, and closets, so one may also settle into a wilderness home. Directly behind the campsite Olaus had chosen there was a little gap in the hillside, in the midst of the forest, where a small beaver pond lay quiet and shining black; but just south of this the hillside was steep and deeply, darkly clothed with trees, and a tiny stream came tumbling down over mossy steps through masses of wild plants, and leapt out into the quiet meadow grass beside our tent. Before it reached the meadow it spilled over a fallen tree trunk, so that it gave us its song continually and also gave us a bucketful of sweet mountain water in an instant.

We had three tents, one for the boys, one for us and the children, one for Grandma, which also contained the little Yukon stove—spaced so that we all had some privacy, and all pitched so that they had some shade for hot days and yet faced the sunny meadow. But the focus of that camp home, as I remember it, was a huge fallen log. In other days trees must have grown larger in Jackson Hole, for this log was more than four feet thick at its base; it lay across the front of our campsite, about 15 feet from the tents and at the very edge of the meadow, and I am sure its presence was Olaus's reason for setting up camp right there. Near its end, he cut down halfway through and leveled the cutoff, making a seat wide enough for the two little people to sit there, a flattened spot on the top of the log at each side forming their "tables." Farther along the log, opposite the campfire, Olaus built a cupboard of split poles for me, atop the log, and this territory became my kitchen. About the campfire and grate on which I cooked were arranged other chunks of other logs for seats or small tables. Back beside our tent a clothesline was strung between trees. Home was complete.

And Grandma and the children could not wait. While Olaus initiated the two boys into the methods of picketing horses, out in the meadow, there followed the little blue-eyed lady, graying hair drawn back in a tight bun, long pleated wool skirt almost to her ankles, topped by a red sweater; and Martin and Joanne in their blue coveralls. They had to see what the new home was like. As I worked in my domain, unpacking dishes and food from the panniers, starting a mulligan of meat and fresh vegetables, I glanced now and then over the meadow.

The little stream wound here and there and all about like Tennyson's brook, and only a few yards from the tents, at one side, it flowed flatly over a sandy place; here the children were down on their knees, picking up little stones, handing them to Grandma, who loved rocks and couldn't resist collecting them.

"Look, Grandma, here's one that looks like a dinosaur!" I heard Martin say.

I stood a moment looking across the meadow to the low hills on the opposite side, beyond Whetstone Creek. Above the ranks of dark evergreen and lighter aspen, one flat-topped ridge dropped steeply to the forest in a bold scree of naked gravel, warm brown in color, and on this the setting sun behind our camp was casting its brilliant light, turning the brown into gold. Olaus and the boys (hungry, I knew!) were walking back through the tall green meadow grasses and bright flowers. Time to wash up, to gather about the fire for food and talk. It was a quiet golden moment. We had arrived safely. Martin came running: "Look, Mommy, here's a rock that's all red!"

These were our days: awake and up soon after daylight. While I started breakfast, Olaus helped the children get dressed, heated some water, and persuaded them to wash their faces and hands in the camp washbasin. By that time I could dish out their bowls of mush and start cooking pancakes or bannock for the rest of us. Soon after breakfast Olaus and the boys would depart either afoot or on the horses for a day of field work, carrying sandwiches, cookies, and an orange apiece in the saddlebags. Grandma and the children and I would be left in camp, and would busy ourselves about the camp chores. Cook more dried fruit for supper and for the next breakfast; plan what the dinner could be; wash the breakfast dishes (this was a task Grandma took on), wash some clothes, heating the water in another dishpan over the fire, rinse them in the creek, hang the clothes to dry; keep an ear out for the sound of the children's voices. If

I could hear *their* prattle above the steady prattle of the little stream, I knew all was well. There was nothing in these woods to hurt them.

After lunch and a nap or rest for all four of us, we usually went on a little exploration of our own, and we came to know and visit many special places. Across the meadow, down the main trail and over to Whetstone Creek itself, there was a place the children named "the sand place" where the stream widened and was shallow and had down logs across it and lovely clean sand and pretty rocks, and here we built sand castles. Farther down the trail, where it skirted the base of the slope, was "the dirt place." Here in a washed-out bank the soil was like clay, and all sorts of tiny caves and shelves and doll-size rooms could be excavated, to be occupied by animals and people made from sticks and cones and whisps of grass.

In all this play Grandma joined with no difficulty, but her chief joy was the profusion of wild flowers, and always she came back with a bouquet of geraniums, asters, monkshood, and larkspur, so that we always had flowers in an empty jam jar on top of the rustic cupboard. And while we strolled and looked, and became friends with squirrels, chipmunks, and jays, she taught us songs from her Norwegian childhood, and told us stories of her girlhood summers spent in the "seter," or high mountain pastures, with the milk cows from her family's farm. Here at the forks of Whetstone Creek in Wyoming she was reliving all those days, and I think she was very happy.

When we returned from our afternoon expeditions it was always time to begin preparing supper, and plenty of it. Usually

Olaus and the boys would return at the proper time, but many evenings it grew late, became dark, and Grandma and I, having fed the children and put them to bed, would sit by the fire and wait, and talk. I learned that for all her love of the out-of-doors and the hills, she was also imbued, way down deep, with a great respect amounting almost to fear of all natural forces—wind, storm, dark, thunder, and lightning—and of accidents that could happen in the wilderness. Perhaps this was a natural inheritance from the rigorous life of generations of her people in Norway. Anyway, when darkness began to fall she began to worry. I would laughingly tell her it was awfully nice of her to do all the worrying, then I didn't need to do any. I had truly battled this thing on my honeymoon and determined not to let it become dominant in me. Yet I was of course just as happy and relieved as she was when, far up the trail, through the darkness, we would hear a coyote howl. A very fine imitation of a real coyote, yet somehow there was Olaus's voice in it! And always Grandma's first remark thereafter would be: "We must get the food ready."

This also I am sure traced back to the age-old Norwegian attitude that the man was somehow the important one, and that he must be fed promptly and abundantly whenever he appeared on the scene. When we lived in town, and Olaus would be out for the day, the moment she saw his panel truck turn in over the cattleguard she would invariably call to me: "Have you anything to eat for your man?"

Many women have asked me: "How did you manage the children way off there in the hills?"

Well, all I can say is that it was simpler there than in town. They were well fed, and because they were busy in the open air every moment, their appetites were wonderful; they grew and were brown and never had a sick moment that I can recall. Their clothes were so simple—underwear, socks, sturdy shoes, coveralls of blue or tan denim, cloth hats to protect them a bit from the sun—there was no ironing. Their play was no problem; they were busy from morning till night with places and objects they found right there in the wilderness. I think that the only phase of camping which bothered me in any way was so much stooping, over the campfire and over the dishpan on the log where I scrubbed out the clothes, and over the little stream where I sloshed them well and wrung them out. It is well for a camping mother to have a strong and limber back!

At the same time I had no hardwood floors to wax and polish; no furniture to dust, no telephone to answer, no parties or committee meetings to attend; no problems of neighborhood children's squabbles (though we never had these in the town of Jackson either); no dresses to starch, no trousers to press; and so on and so on.

But perhaps above all this was the plain fact that camp life suited me; it was just naturally no trouble for me to settle into it. I have always felt that if a woman does not "take" to this kind of life she should not be expected to do so, and should not be criticized if she stays behind in town. If she goes unwillingly, *making* herself be a camper, she is not likely to be a carefree cheerful companion. I do think that if a man plans a career that is to take him into the wilderness, he should bear this in mind when getting acquainted with young women; if he *could* happen to fall in love with one who was harmonious with the out-of-doors, it would be a fortunate situation.

Some days Olaus and the boys did not go far afield searching for bands of wapiti and studying their food habits, but stayed in camp to put up small specimens, to replenish wood supplies, to write notes, to repair gear. So it was that they were all in camp the morning the children had a visitor. Martin and Joanne had discovered and pre-empted for themselves a little nook between the tents and the beaver pond, in the thick woods. They called this their playhouse—it was a sort of natural room outlined by down logs, and here were their play cupboards and rooms, and their play companions, where they enacted all sorts of adventures. But one morning they came tearing out of there and over to camp, all breathless and upset, crying: "Mommy, Daddy, a moose, a moose in our playhouse!"

As soon as Olaus could quiet them and get the story from Martin, he and the boys quickly walked back to the pond and there sure enough was a big bull moose with half-grown antlers, feeding in the pond. It appeared that he had simply walked right through the "playhouse," almost brushing against the children. Trying to get the details, Olaus asked Martin: "Was the moose looking at you?"

"No, his back was looking at us!"

This was the pattern of our days on Whetsone Creek; this was the kind of adventure that punctuated the pattern. Most of them were happy episodes. I remember Martin and Joanne squealing with delight as Olaus stood them in the shallow part of the little creek, where the water was warmed by the hot mountain sunshine, and soaped them and scrubbed them and rinsed them—a hilarious game. I remember hot days of July when we sought the shade of the trees or the tents and many camp chores were left to the cool of the long evenings, and when the wild strawberries ripened and Grandma and the children went happily stooping and crawling through the grass out in the meadow to gather them. Then I would bake some biscuit, we would mash the berries through a little sieve, since they were too tiny to hull, and that evening we would have strawberry shortcake.

I remember, too, waking early one morning at a strange rustling sound. Glancing with half an eye at the partly open tent flap, I thought I saw a red and white Royal salt carton waving about in mid-air. What kind of joke were the boys up to now? Was I dreaming? I poked Olaus and whispered: "Look, please, what on earth . . . ?"

Olaus, like most outdoorsmen, I think, slept soundly, but when wakened was instantly alert. He slid quickly over and lifted the flap a bit. "I thought so! My gosh, where's my camera?"

A venturesome porcupine had wandered into camp, found with delight something that tasted salty on the outside, chewed into the end, stuck his head in to lick the delicious stuff in the bottom, and then couldn't get his head out again! Weaving desperately and blindly all over camp, he was trying to get rid of that horrible bonnet. By now the children and Grandma were fascinated spectators and Olaus went over and wakened the boys. For ten minutes he and they pursued the poor creature, taking pictures, and then finally devised a means of freeing him by poking repeatedly at the salt box with a long thin pole. No one wanted to get too close to our visitor. This episode gave the children something to discuss and to re-enact all day long in the playhouse.

Camp life does not slide along on a smooth monotonous level any more than life in town does. One morning Olaus found his usually amiable wife confronting him with fire in her eyes: "If this thing happens once more, you'll have no cook in camp. I'll take the children and go back to town, and I mean it!"

Back in the trees behind Grandma's tent there was another large down log, which had been adopted by Olaus and the boys as the "laboratory" where Olaus was teaching them to put up museum specimens, mice and shrews caught in the trap line the boys put out each evening. The skins had to be "poisoned" against future insect invasion by brushing them with arsenic powder on a cotton swab held in forceps. Olaus kept the arsenic in a piece of rubber sheeting and had of course cautioned the boys about how careful a scientist must be to put this carefully away after each session of skinning; it was to be put in the large metal tackle box which was the skinning kit, and locked in. Twice I had happened to find the rubber sheet still spread out open on the log, and no boys around.

I never knew what Olaus said to the boys that morning after my explosion, but I never found the arsenic on the log again. Maybe they felt they wouldn't care to do their own cooking.

One morning I heard Fletcher calling me from behind Grandma's tent: "Mrs. Murie, I think you had better come look at this."

There stood Joanne in her blue coveralls beside the half crate of eggs that Olaus had brought up on his biweekly trip to Moran for supplies, carefully packed on the gentle mule. Joanne, a few days before, had been intrigued with peeling some hard-boiled eggs I had fixed for their lunch. Now she had found a whole boxful of lovely eggs to peel. Only the first one didn't peel very well; in fact it went right down the front of her blue coveralls. Well, try another one—and another. By the time Fletcher had discovered her she had "peeled" about eight; by the time I got there she had peeled four more, to make a round dozen. Because he was so amused by her serious, businesslike manner—sticking her little thumb into the shell, trying to pick off a piece of shell, losing the egg down her front, picking up another—he couldn't bear to stop the show!

September came, with frosty mornings and frosty nights, and blazing-hot middays. The boys were gone; the family was alone on Whetstone Creek. Olaus wanted to stay as late into the fall as he could, to get the transition on food habits and to continue to study the rutting season of the wapiti. With the cooling of the weather, camp was rearranged and consolidated. In the larger tent we made room for Grandma's bed on one side, ours on the other, the children's side by side at the head of ours at the back of the tent. At the front Olaus made a cupboard arrangement from the wooden pannier boxes; the tent flap was lifted at one side, a fly stretched across to the big log, the little stove installed there, and our supply boxes and duffle boxes arranged and covered with more canvas so that the tent was enlarged into a pretty snug home in case of storm. We knew there would have to be some storms; the whole summer had been too perfect. When we had gone to town to see the boys off and get more supplies, we had also brought back a few toys for the children, and crayons and tablets and books, some reading material for ourselves, and Olaus's painting supplies plus three big canvas boards, so he could get on with a commission he had received for three color plates for a scientific work. All this in an 8 × 10 foot tent. All things are possible, as we soon found.

About the middle of the month Olaus declared a "family

holiday." It was a fine clear morning. We would all take a hike up the main creek above the forks for the day. He had been teaching Martin to cast a fly with his little fishing rod. Maybe Martin could catch us some fish, and we could all see what the country up that way looked like.

Into the rucksack Olaus had given me for our honeymoon in Alaska I packed some lunch and the children's sweaters, and we set off merrily. By this time Grandma had taught us two or three Norwegian songs, and Olaus of course knew them already, so we sang in Norwegian as we trudged along: "Here are we, a lusty flock; of good spirits and singing have we a-plenty; in the heights among the mountain peaks; in the deeps where waterfalls roar; let the way go where it will, we wander on with song and play."

Above the forks the trail was only a game trail, with many down logs across it, but these the children considered great fun, and the high dry Wyoming air had so improved Grandma's knee rheumatism that she was able to get over obstacles pretty well, and found something interesting at every turn of the trail. By noon Olaus figured we were nearly four miles from camp; by the time we made the return trip, that would be eight miles for our two-year-old, so we stopped on a sunny slope under some pine trees, ate our lunch, and the two "men" went down the creek to fish. Never willing to miss anything of interest, Joanne went along too, though she was told she would have to "be quiet and not talk" if they were to catch any fish. Grandma and I were content to relax in the shade and wait.

They returned in an hour, quite triumphant. We could hear the happy voices chattering away before they came round the bend, and then Martin held up to us proudly three nice, eating-size trout. We started down the slope to join them. Behind me I heard a gasp, and turned to see Grandma lying on the pine needles with one knee bent under her. Pine needles are slippery, and of course in falling it was her bad rheumatic knee that had been sprained. Olaus came running, lifted her, and sat her with back against a tree while he examined her and found nothing broken, only a bad sprain. "I'm dizzy," she whispered in Norwegian. I dug into the rucksack and found one orange left from lunch, cut a hole in it, told her to suck it, and this seemed to revive her.

Olaus and I looked at each other. No need for words. We were four miles from camp, with a disabled elderly woman, two small children, three small trout. The children were standing wide-eyed, for once speechless. Olaus turned to them:

"You kiddies sit down over here under this tree and be quiet and rest while Mommy and I fix Grandma so we can carry her to camp; and don't worry, we'll get back all right, but you folks will have to walk, so you'd better rest now."

He turned to me: "See what you have in your rucksack that we can use for a sort of seat. I'm going up here and find some poles."

He walked away. I looked at Grandma. The color had come back into her face, and she smiled at me. "Just rest," I said. "We'll get you back to camp all right. We can be so glad nothing is broken; and I'm glad you only weigh 103 pounds! Now, if *I* had been the one who slipped, what would you and Olaus have done? Does it hurt terribly?"

"No, not when I hold it still."

In the rucksack I found four large flour sacks, left from some previous trip, and a length of cheesecloth from Olaus's skinning kit. In its outside pockets were a wad of heavy twine and two bootlaces, and in my shirt pocket I discovered two large safety pins. I took off the big red bandana from my head; that could be used for something surely. Olaus returned with two slender pine poles and set to work.

In half an hour we were moving homeward down the trail. Olaus carried the heavy ends of the poles; he had taken off his wool shirt and used it as a sling over his shoulder to take some of the strain. Directly in front of him sat his mother on a seat made of flour sacks tied together, then tied to the poles; the uninjured leg was tied in a short sling almost on the level with the poles, but the injured knee could not be treated in this way. The only way she could stand the pain was with the leg hanging down from the knee, so Olaus had made a longer sling of cheesecloth in which she rested her heel. If nothing jarred or touched the foot or leg, she felt little pain.

At the front of this homemade litter I walked between the poles. Behind us came the children. I had put their sweaters on them, and Martin carried the fishing rod and the three trout in a forked stick; he *must* take his fish back to camp! There had been a few cookies left from lunch, and these the children had eaten while they rested and watched us make the litter. It was by now nearly four o'clock. "I guess it will be after dark when we get back," said Olaus, "but it's full moon tonight, so we should be all right anyway."

Now the down logs in the game trail were both a boon

and a challenge. A challenge because when we came to one we must lift the litter high enough so that the hanging foot would clear the log—and this took some doing. A boon because when we had to stop to rest we simply rested our passenger on a log, with her foot hanging. Olaus had the heavy end, but I had the part which had to be lifted high at each obstruction. I think those blessed children really saved us. They made a game of it. The litter was a choo-choo train, and every time we had to stop to rest it was a wreck. Every few minutes they would call to us: "When you goin' to have another wreck?"

In a little while we came to the first crossing of the creek, but Olaus had already figured it all out. We lifted Grandma, who was by now convinced she was going to survive, and her lively spirit and sense of humor were rising to the occasion of which she was the star. We stood her upright, I holding her so she could stand on the good leg. Olaus got in front of her; she clasped her hands about his neck. Bending far over, with her hanging straight down his back, he carried her to the other side, where I would be waiting to hold her again. Then he returned for the litter; then for one child, then for the other.

We had to go through this performance three times, and by the time we did it the third time I was going on sheer nerve, or so I thought; every muscle seemed to be crying aloud. Darkness had fallen and with it had come clouds to obscure the full moon we had so counted on. We moved in almost complete darkness. Grandma was very quiet and I knew she was reaching exhaustion. But the children were still coming along, uncomplaining though slow. As in a daze I heard Olaus call back to Martin: "Keep close to 'Bay Sis'; don't let her get too far behind—you are the big helper, you know."

Then I heard Olaus say: "We're going to make it—just a little farther, Mardy, can you do it? This is the wide place in the creek, and I can see the meadow ahead, and see, there's a little moon showing, at last." A good thing, too. I was beginning to wonder if I could find the trail across the meadow.

Almost like a dream, the big log, and the gleam of the white tent, and one more great effort while we got our patient into the tent, unlaced her shoes, got her into bed. My arms were trembling uncontrollably from those hours of pulled muscles. Olaus and I sort of collapsed against each other for one great moment of relief, but then, where were the children? "Here I am," said Martin, and handed the trout to Olaus. But where is Joanne? Olaus started out toward the meadow, calling, and then we heard a little voice: "Here I am!"

Neither of us would ever forget the sound of that baby voice from the darkness: "Here I am!"

6

The Black Horse

{{ O·M }}

When old Bob Stanton died in 1927 he left a little white mule, a
black horse, a couple of saddles, and other miscellaneous pack
outfit—his entire estate, with no heirs to claim it. It was offered
for sale to pay a hospital bill, and I put in a very modest bid;
I think it was $125. All I was interested in was getting a horse.
To my surprise, when the bids were opened I learned that I
was the owner of the livestock and the gear.

Here I was, new to Jackson Hole, and new to horses.
Fresh from dog-sledding in the north, I found myself face to
face with a new travel technique, face to face with the care and
management of horses. I knew enough to realize my own inadequate judgment of horses, and relied on newfound friends
to give me advice. I asked Henry Crabtree if he knew Bob
Stanton's black horse. He squinted his eyes, looked judicious,
and said: "Oh, I believe he's a pretty good horse. He may be a
little bit snaky."

Little did I realize the significance of that last remark. "A little snaky" was to mean several seasons of petty annoyances, laughable incidents, and downright grief. We never knew the horse's real name, and always called him simply "The Black." It has seemed suitable in every respect.

After my first experience with The Black I asked advice from several knowledgeable cowboy friends. I explained that the horse was perfectly all right, easy to ride, and all that, but that when he was loose it was next to impossible to catch him. I explained that when I was out in the hills I had only two or three head of horses, was inexperienced, and naturally there would be no corral to drive them into. Several looked at The Black, among them of course Almer, and they all agreed that obviously someone must have abused him about the head and had made him hard to touch. And a variety of remedies were offered.

I tried them all. One was to attach a length of chain to a front foot. A sure-fire cure, I was told. The Black grazed in a pasture, dragging the heavy chain. When I approached him, off he went in a panic, lashing himself cruelly with that chain. This punishment was supposed to teach him to take it easy, so as not to be hurt. Almer had said that most horses would learn to stand after such treatment. Not The Black.

In camp at the head of Arizona Creek in 1928 we picketed our horses by a front foot and let them drag a fairly heavy log in the meadow to give them greater range in their grazing. One day Adolph and I and Mardy's young brother Louis went out into the meadow to bring in all three horses for a day's trip. I felt I should tackle The Black myself, and quietly, very quietly approached him with his halter concealed behind my back. Off he dashed like a racehorse from the starting post; and when he came to the end of his rope he did not stop but kept right on, with the heavy log, over four feet long, bouncing wildly after him, straight up toward camp at the edge of the timber.

In camp, Mardy was in our tent kneeling by a washbasin of warm water, giving fourteen-month-old Joanne her bath. She heard shouts, and the thunder of hoofs with a queer thumping sound approaching the tent. All she had time to do was crouch over the baby, shielding her with her own body, while the pounding of hoofs and the thumping went by, just outside the tent wall. How that bouncing log escaped being tangled in the guy ropes of the tent and bringing the whole thing down we shall never understand, but The Black tore right on into the woods until he became all snarled up in a thicket of young pine trees and had to stop.

Somehow we came to another summer, this time on Whetstone Creek, and we still had The Black. The horses had wintered on the Elk Refuge and the The Black had seemed a bit more amenable that spring, and I had hopes he might be outgrowing his malady. But one morning when I was approaching him I saw that wild panicky look come into his eyes, and off he dashed, the picket rope broke, and he galloped off toward Wildcat Peak. I quickly saddled Lady, the always dependable mare, who could outwalk and outrun any of the other horses, and we went after him. Sooner or later I would wear him down, get him cornered somewhere, and get my hands on him. This time when I finally caught him my exasperation had worked itself up to quite a pitch. I took the saddle off Lady, knowing she would follow, got on him, and muttering: "Now then, if you want to go, then *go!*" I lashed him furiously and rode him all the way back to camp at top speed.

When I walked up to the tents after picketing the horses again I confess I felt a little shamefaced when I was met with the quiet, half-amused remark: "And what was that exhibition supposed to mean?"

"Gosh, Mardy, a fellow has to let go *sometimes!*"

The year before, in our early career with The Black, Ade and I were in camp on Upper Gravel Creek. We had with us a few extra horseshoes and nails, but for some reason had no other horseshoeing equipment. And of course it was The Black that cast a couple of shoes.

Now, we knew how to put moccasins on sled dogs when their feet got sore, but neither of us had ever shod a horse. We put off this job for a few days and rode the horse barefoot. But the trails were rocky and the hoofs were wearing down; in fact, they were wearing away on the sides and beginning to look like horny claws. The decision had to be made. "We've got to do it tonight. But let's give him a good long ride today so he won't feel so lively. Maybe then we can handle him."

In addition to his other qualities, we had learned that The Black was sensitive about his feet and had a tendency to kick.

I could imagine the chuckle from Charlie Brown, the blacksmith in town, had he been able to look in on us that evening. First, how does the blacksmith get the horse's foot

into his lap? I had watched Charlie many times—it's funny how details escape your memory. But somehow we solved that one without too much trouble.

So I had the hoof in my lap while Ade held the horse's head and talked kindly to him to keep his attention off his hind leg. We knew that we had to shave down the hoof to make it level. We had seen Charlie do that with the farrier's knife, and clip off projecting edges with big nippers, and file the hoof down with a great rasp. But we had none of these tools. I picked away with my pocket knife. Have you ever tried to cut a horse's hoof to size with a small knife? I was amazed at the hoof's hardness. The places that were soft didn't need cutting. The projections were unusually hard. The result was a compromise. If I could get three points fairly level the shoe ought to hold the weight of the horse, I reasoned.

The next question was the nails. We had noticed that the tip was beveled off on one side. Should the beveled side face out or in? We reasoned that it should face in, so as to prevent the nail from slanting in to the "quick." This proved to be right. We had no hammer, but used the edge of an eight-inch file to pound with. Somehow, with the file and a rock we managed to clinch the nails.

Many a time I had to let down the hoof, for a fresh start. I tried my best to make the horse feel that an expert was handling his feet, that we wouldn't stand for any monkey business. I wanted to discourage any inclination he might have to kick (and the symptoms were there several times). If he only knew! What could he have thought of that tentative nibbling with the pocket knife, the awkward tapping with the file? Did he not remember the firmness of Charlie, the positive driving of the nails, the authentic clang of iron, on those former trips to the blacksmith?

Maybe we were just lucky. We got the shoes nailed on, and the ordeal was over. Moreover, they stayed on, and for a long time, and the horse had no further trouble with his feet.

But this was only the beginning of our troubles with him. The next autumn Mardy and I were confronted with the problem of getting Mother, with her sprained knee, down to the end of the road and the car. We had spent two more weeks in camp after her accident. I had gone to Moran and called Dr. Huff in Jackson, and we had treated the knee as he advised and it was much better. But we knew she could not walk four miles, and here it was almost the first of October and we had already had one snowstorm.

I made a couple of trips down to the road with camp gear and had no trouble, and on a nice sunny morning we were all packed and ready to leave with the final load. We had made the best plan we could think of. With Mardy's help I got the mule and the bay horse Tony packed, and that morning The Black had been easy to approach. Once caught, he was always gentle—so we thought. We were short one pack saddle, and I managed somehow with plenty of rope to load the big duffle bag and the sleeping bags onto the riding saddle on The Black.

When all was ready I brought Lady up and got her to stand very close to the big down log outside the tent. Then while Mardy held her head, I lifted Mother into the saddle, arranged the stirrups so that her bandaged knee was comfortable, then went over and loosed the two other horses and the mule from the trees where they were tied. I took the mare's halter and started walking, leading her. She had a very smooth gait, and Mother said her knee didn't hurt, and I knew the mule and Tony would follow along after the mare. I looked back as we reached the middle of the meadow and all three were following along quietly. I waved back to Mardy.

During those days in camp I had spent my spare time working on a large oil painting of elk in a mountain scene, to fulfill a commission I had received for a color plate for a book. I had carried the big canvas board all wrapped in paper and corrugated cardboard up from the road head; there was no other way. And now Mardy would have to carry it down. She said she would pick up the last scraps around camp, to leave it perfectly tidy, and then would start down the trail with painting under one arm, rucksack with lunch and the last odds and ends on her back, and the two children trailing along—but it would be a slow trip.

All went well with my part of the expedition for almost three miles. We were in the last small meadow before the trail climbed through some small hills and dropped through lodgepole pine forest to the end of the road. I knew Mother was greatly relieved to be getting down toward town and her own room and bed and care, but she said her knee felt all right, and we were reminiscing about old days in Moorhead and some of my boyhood friends, when I heard a commotion behind us and looked back. I knew that Tony sometimes bucked, but to see The Black bucking wildly all over that meadow was like a nightmare; then I saw that one of my fancy World War I Balloon Corps knots must have come untied and a rope end was hitting him on the neck; and as I turned, Tony was getting into action also.

At the edge of the meadow just ahead of us was a lone small pine and I quickly tied Lady to this and ran for the meadow. I got to Tony, and when I had my hand on his halter he quieted down, but was trembling. And we were all watching The Black. There was nothing I could do about him. He was putting on a full-scale rodeo by himself, trying to get rid of all the things that were bothering him. And he did. First the sleeping-bag roll came loose and fell to the grass; then the old duffle bag split neatly right across the middle and flew off in two pieces, scattering clothing all over the meadow; finally the other roll of bedding slipped out of its ropes.

And then The Black disappeared from my view. With

the saddle still on, and with ropes trailing behind, he galloped through the timber eastward. All this time I was worried for fear the incomparable Lady might become infected with the excitement and start moving about or rearing, with Mother on her. The only thing I could do was get back there quickly and go on to the road. Fortunately, on this occasion Tony's allegiance was more to the mare than to The Black, and he followed after the mule.

Two hours later, striding up the trail with rifle in hand and leading Tony, I met the family. Mardy, having seen the scattered belongings back in the little meadow, had a worried look on her face, but it changed to near terror when she suddenly met me round a bend in the trail. She told me later she had never seen such a look on my face. I said no word of greeting.

"Have you seen that black horse anywhere? If I find him I'm going to shoot him!"

But they had not seen him, and I did not find him. I could not take time this day to search for him. I could only gather up the spilled outfit, pack it on Tony, and return to the car, and by that time dusk was falling, I had cooled off a bit, we were all feeling thankful to be on our way home, and the problem of The Black would have to be taken care of later.

So he was spared, and since I had told all the ranchers and the forest ranger in this district about him, he was recognized when he showed up in Roy Lozier's hunting camp among his horses, minus saddle and ropes.

Like most of us, The Black had contrasting qualities.

Once you had a halter on him he was the gentlest of souls; he was suddenly transformed from a wild mustang, from "the bronco who could not be broken of dancing" to a tired, solemn, mature personality. He followed Lady sedately, never showing any spirit, in fact even stumbling at times. But with all this he was a good-looking animal, well formed, shiny black.

So we came to late fall of 1932, when I was again in the Upper Yellowstone country studying the fall migration of the wapiti, and alone. I was camped at Bridger Lake and kept the horses picketed in the big meadow. I had found by this time that if I kept Lady picketed, Tony the bay and The Black would stay nearby, and of course the mule never left her.

My mother had a belief, brought from Norway, that in the fall at the equinox all creatures become restless; there was a troublesome spirit riding through the land. As nearly as I can come in English to the Norwegian name for it, it would be called "The Ride of the Berserks."

Perhaps The Black was infected with this spirit. One morning as I was cooking breakfast in my tent I was suddenly impelled to open the flap and see how everything was, out in the meadow. I looked out upon a lowering sky, a dark day with the feel of snow in the air. And out in the meadow I saw The Black, walking up close to Tony, then starting off, then walking up close to him again.

Suddenly they both started off, The Black in the lead; they crossed the meadow to the south side, found the down-country trail, and started along, and their whole demeanor told me that they were *leaving*. The mule, of course, paid them no attention; she was standing near the mare.

I knew right then that this was the last act in the The Black drama. I put on my coat, took my rifle and saddle and went out and saddled Lady. The others were no match for her, and before long we caught them up, going steadily down the trail. I passed them, went ahead; they fell in behind. In a few minutes I picked a spot, left the trail, led them over into a small stand of pines well away from the trail.

There I left the Black Horse. Lady, Tony, the mule, and I returned to camp.

7

Beaver Dick

{{ O·M }}

It was really a pleasant October day. An early snowfall had melted away and it was quite warm, but the recent glory of the aspens was gone; the trees were bare and gray, heavy clouds were rolling up over the mountains, spilling over on our side; there was a sound of the intermittent wind in the trees which affected me strangely. I experienced that peculiar sense of insecurity that comes over me on some occasions, especially in the fall. Perhaps barometric pressures do affect us, with wind and certain atmospheric conditions. I vaguely thought of the creatures of primitive times, man himself when he first ventured forth into the realm of thought and reflection. How did this world seem to those early ones, who were still so much at the mercy of wind and snow and the many forces they had not yet learned to understand?

Somehow, pondering all this as I stood watching the wind-tossing of the cottonwoods, I got to thinking about some of the early settlers in the Rockies, in Jackson Hole, and from this vantage point in history my thoughts roved back to the earlier day, the day of exploration, the day filled with hardships and exultation, hope, ambition, strife, all of these in the rugged terms of the early frontier. Beaver Dick Leigh, for example, hunting "ground hogs," shooting antelope, providing for his family, then suffering bereavement under the most cruel conditions.

Leigh Lake. Jenny Lake. Only names to us now. But what did they mean to the firstcomers? How did *they* interpret this particular landscape?

We are so apt to fall into the habit of seeing a lake or a mountain in the thin "tourist" aspect. A worthy view, to be sure; I have full sympathy for the woman who was busy fussing with the filter on her lens, adjusting the tripod, meticulously studying the light meter. That group of pine limbs high up was a thoughtful arrangement, framing in silhouette the waters of Jenny Lake and the mountains beyond.

I enjoy being with the crowds at Jenny Lake sometimes, watching them snapping pictures, busying themselves about their camp, setting out with binoculars on the trails. People at their best, in a place of inspiration. But I wonder if we cannot take back with us something lasting and rich if we look beyond the pictorial beauty and try to absorb some of that intangible quality of mountains and lake that enters the soul of the pioneer, that comes with understanding and interpretation of what we see. Jenny. Leigh. These can very well mean to us much more than two blue gems at the foot of the mountains.

The evening before this day of my October reflections, a group of friends had been gathered at our fireplace and we had discussed the early travelers that our fragments of recorded history for Jackson Hole told us about. Now, as I looked out on the autumn landscape I recalled a significant early diary of which I had made a copy years before, and I was impelled to go to the filing case and find it, to leaf through the copied pages again.

These two beautiful lakes at the foot of the Tetons, Jenny and Leigh, are visited each year by thousands of people, and thousands of pictures are taken from their shores. Behind the naming of these lakes lies a fascinating and virile history going back into the past century.

In 1872 C. Hart Merriam, then a sixteen-year-old boy, was here in the valley on the famous Hayden Survey. Later he became a doctor, then a biologist, one of the founders of natural-history research in our country, the first Chief of the United States Biological Survey. When he was over eighty years old, Mardy, Donald, and I had the pleasure of being his house guests in Washington, D.C. He told us much about his early explorations in the West, and showed us letters and the diary of Richard Leigh, known as Beaver Dick, who had been a guide to the Hayden party through part of its travels. His son, Dick, Jr., and young Hart Merriam, the same age, had shared a bedroll during this part of the party's travels. The diaries and letters were written in a very fine, small, perfect hand, which is puzzling since the spelling is that of a totally uneducated man. A few years ago, Dr. Merriam's daughter and son-in-law, Mr. and Mrs. M. W. Talbot, made these records available to me.

Richard Leigh was an Englishman who married an Indian wife who was apparently comely and intelligent and capable, and the marriage was a happy one. Her name was Jenny; hence the names of the two lakes in what is now Grand Teton National Park.

Actually, Beaver Dick and his family lived on the Idaho side of the Teton Mountains, in the country known as Teton Basin, but all of Jackson Hole was familiar hunting ground for him. Even then, in the 1870's and 1880's, venturesome and wealthy trophy hunters journeyed that far west, and Beaver Dick was one of the region's chief guides. Excerpts from Beaver Dick's diary bring to us after all the intervening years a picture of life in those early days, a decade or more before Jackson Hole itself had any permanent settlers:

19th May, 1875. We [his son Dick and he] packed the elk meat and skin on our horses and started for home. we ad traveld 4 or 5 mills when my riden mare got frightened at a chicken that flew up under her nose. she jumped 7 or 8 feet one side nearly unhorsing me and spraned my thumb so that it swelled and paned badly with a roape that i was leading a pack horse with. i was so vexed that i truck her over the head with my gunn. about a mile further on i went to shoot a ground hog [no doubt what we call woodchuck or rockchuck today] when I saw my gunn barrol was bent something like an indians bow. i lade it on a large rock and took out my little ax and went to work to streghten it out. in ½ an hour i got hur to shoot within 2 or 3 inches of the mark at 75 steps so i left it alone at that until i would get home. we got to mr. Lyons at noone, left them some meat and fowl we had killed expresly for the old people, took dinner with them. while packing my horses Alven and John Lyons [sons of the old people] came to the house and quarald with me and told me that if ever i came around thare agane i should neaver leave there with my life at the same time steping back toward his gun that was hanging on the side of the house. my gunn was outside at the gable end of the house but 3 jumps and she was in my hands and cocked and leveled at his head. Just as he was reaching for his gun. He had mistaken his man this time so he swallowed what he ad sead while looking downe my indians bow gunn. his father took courage at this and demanded his property and told them to leave his premeses but they told him in my presence that he ad nothing that everything was thars and ordered him out of the house. Alven struck his father 5 times in the face and John snatched a duble barl rifall when i turned my gunn on him and made him lay it downe. he sead he was going to shoot me that he was going to shoot the dambd old broot meaning his father if he should strike Alven with a small hammer that he ad taken in his hand to protect himself with. Mistrs Lyons and hur daughter mrs Berry begd me to stay with them and protect them. i told them i had a big family to mantane and if i should stay i wold have to kill Alven and John or they wold kill me so I told the young men that thare father and mother and sister ad cald on me to protect them and i should cirtnly do so and i wold hold them responsible for thare father and mothers lives untill i could get some asistance for them. Alven took a club in his hand abot 4 feet long and 3 inches thrue wile he was cursing and abusing his father and made towards him saying he wold mash him to the ground.

i told him if he struck the old man i wold shoot him. that ended the fuss and me and my son Dick started for home but the sequl is to come yet.

July 12, 1875. Myself and Tom [Lavering] and John [Houge] went to Mr. Lyons at his call and prayers to arest his 2 sons Alven and John Lyons for threts they had made against his life and property. we took them to my camp with charges against them to be turned over to the sherriff of malad city as soone as we can get across the river and take them downe.

July 13. Alven Lyons took the hobls off his horse and let hur go wile we whare eating brexfast. he came to get his saddle and his brothers horse to follow hur. John Houge told him that game wold not win and if he undertook to play a nother trick like that he wold ave to walk to malad and be tyed downe at night in the Bargin. houge went and fetched the mare back. me and Tom went to try to find a ford on the teton river. we could not find a crosing it was very high.

July 14. We took our prisnors and went downe to my boat and puled it on a sled to the mouth of the South Teton. thare we swam our horses and crosed ourselves and sadls in the Boat. after crosing we went 3 miles and camped at scorpen camp a mile above the crator Buttes. hear thare was a Mr. Thomas Davis from montana with 2 hyard men and 2 waggins and a hurd of 4 hundred stock cattle looking for a place to settle. i gave him all the information he required and the use of my Boat to cros the river and look at the country.

July 19th. we got to malad city at 10 o'clock the Cort was in seshun our prisnors was put under Bale one Brother going the others bale for 3 hundred dollars when both of them was not worth one of the Bonds. thay allso put me under 3 hundred dolars Bonds for 6 months for taking my rifall to defend my life when Alven thretened me last may at the same time reaching for his gunn. the law in this section is only a Bilk and God keep me a long ways from it for i shall try and never Bother with sutch law agane. the lyons were well knowne all along the road and the people came out Boldly and sade we ad aught to ave tryed them by Mountain Law.

The diary of Beaver Dick Leigh is of course largely concerned with the business of survival, which was his life, but here and there is a phrase that gives us a feeling of his love of that free life which he had chosen, and his keen observation of and sympathy with the big wild country he lived in, and of his happiness in his family. Trapping was the main occupation, which gave him cash for the few necessities to be bought at the nearest trading post, but all the time there must be hunting for food. I note that during the month of July, 1874, he killed 19 marmots (which we call woodchuck and which he called ground hog or just plain hog), 8 antelope, 5 grouse (ruffed grouse), and 1 sage grouse. On August 4 he wrote:

no beaver catchem. i took a days ride upstreem to the foot of the range. When within 7 or 8 mills of the range i saw a post idaho on one side and wyoming on the other. thair ad beene a survaying party gone thrue 6 or 7 dayes ago that accounts for the fresh Boot tracks that i saw on the 29th of July at the head of falls river. i went 2 or 3 mills further saw nothing to justafy me to take camp up thare kill 2 hogs returne to camp.

Aug. 8 . . . me and Dick went hunting kill one buck antelope while we ware away 2 comrade trappers came along from Jacksons Lake John Renolds and Little Jimmy and ad camp with us. they report nothing to trap or hunt in that vercinaty but bair this seson and they ware so plenty that it was unsafe going the rounds to thare traps. they ware going to Virgina City Montana to sell thare fur and get an outfit of provishons. i gave them half of the antlope i ad killed so as not to detane them as they was out of meet and did not want to stop and hunt eny.

Aug. 9. caught 4 beaver. Renolds and Jimmy moved north. me and Dick went hunting. we saw a large band of antlope and started for them. when geting near to them we saw fresh elk traks we left the antlope and went on thare trale acrost Leigh's Creek close to foot of mountains saw three elk close to the 3 cottonwoods on the little creek betwene Leighs Crk and teton crk in the open country we started for them. dun a grate deele of manuvering to get a shot finly i got a long shot at a Bull. Broke his left hind leg. he started for the swamp. he got a mile and a half the start before Dick came up with the horses. i spranginto the sadle and started for him. i ad run about 2 mills when my riley mare steped into a badger hole and fell unhorsing me and roling over me. my gunn went off as we fell. as soone as i got clere of the mare i jumped up and as soone as she got on hir legs i bounsed into the sadl and was on the run agane but the elk ad got so much the start that he reched the swamp before i could get up with him. i walked around and thrue the swamp. i rased him twice but could not get a shot up to my waste in water and bluegrass and willows very thick. i got tyard and gave him up and started for home a tyard man, met Dick outside the swamp.

Random selections from this diary give us a picture of life in Teton Basin in Idaho in the 1870's:

caught 1 beaver, 1 mink.

Shot 1 doe antlope.

crossed Leigh's creek. we were keene on the lookout for thare was no meet at camp.

it was thundering and lightning one of the heavyst rane storms i ave seene for a long time. it lasted 15 minutes but was very chily the rest of the day.

Dick got into a flock of ducks, killed 4. When we got to camp Jinny and the children ad taken horses and crosed the river to yamp crk. to dig yamp.[1] It is very plenty thare and is a good substitute for potatos. . . . I took 3 traps to set at juncon of Sarvesberry Crk, i pased Jinny and children they ware digging away like good fellows.

rane with heavy thunder and lightning every 2 hours thrue the night betwixt storms the moone wold shine out clere. the heavey clouds commenced to rase to the top of mount moran and the Big Teton. at noone every cloud was gone.

During September of that year, 1874, Beaver Dick and his son took 8 antelope, 1 deer, 1 lynx, 1 goose, 3 sage grouse, 6 ducks. It is clear that meat was the chief item in their diet, and I doubt if any was wasted. From May 1875 until November 5, 1875, they took 28 antelope, 21 deer, 2 elk, 31 marmots—but remember, there was a family of five children to be fed. On October 2 he mentions that a buffalo was sighted by some Indians and wounded, and he says: "This is the first Boflo that as beene seene since the spring of 1871."

---

[1] Yampa, *Perideridia gairdneri*, one of the carrot family. One of the best wild plant foods of the Rocky Mountain region, it has a parsnip flavor raw. Cooked, it is sweet and mealy. The small, sweet-potato-shaped tubers are the parts used. (Information taken from Craighead's *Field Guide to Rocky Mountain Flowers.*)

It is apparent, and interesting to me, that the elk were in those days not as numerous as they are today, for he mentions them seldom, and when a band was sighted they were immediately the object of an intensive chase.

Thus far in this chapter we have looked back, through the pages of his diary, at the happier years of Beaver Dick's life. The darker chapter which followed is revealed in a letter dated April 1, 1877, to Dr. Josiah Curtis, who must have been one of the Eastern hunters Beaver Dick had guided into the mountains at some time. An original copy of this, handwritten, was also sent to Dr. Merriam.

My Dear Frend:

i set downe to give you an account of myself and my lost famley. i moved up to the elbo of the teton river on the 25th day of Aprl 1876. thare i built a log cabin and fenced me a farme and rased some little fegetables. i also built a horse corall and hay corall and put up 6 ton of hay in it. i also went and packed Tom Lavering and his pardner and thare camp and skins out of the mountains. . . . On the first day of August Tom and my son Richard started on a traping trip up the middle river. wile me and my wife hauled in the hay tom and dick found nothing worth traping came back the last of august and me and Tom went and traped the north fork of Snake with the Boat. at my wife's request i took hur and famley into camp like about the 25 of September. we traped downe to a mile of my old winter cabin at the juncon of the teton river. when we got thrue traping my wife sead she wold like to spend the winter in our old cabin as she might want some asistance during the winter and our new place was too

far off from enybody so i moved my famley and household
goods to the old cabin at hur request. Tom built a cabin near
me and then we went downe to Warrins store on Blackfoot
for suplys on the 2nd of November. i caught a bad cold and
sufered from my old complaint whatever it is. on the 11th of
November we passed Humphys camp at the point of rocks 2
miles from John Adousie's place. Humphy's Indian wife came
out and asked me for some bread. i told hur i ad none baked,
and we went on 6 miles to the foot of the Crator Buttes and
camped. wile we were eating supper by the light of the fire
humphy's wife and daughter 3 years old came and sade
Humphy had comited sueside and her and hur child were
starving.

we gave hur something to eate and blankets to sleep in.
the next morning she came to ware we were crosing our suplys
with the boat and sade she wanted to go over the river to see
my wife. i put her acrost when we ad got everything acrost
we went on home. my wife told me that Humphy's father ad
died and his mother ad broke out in the face with little bumps.
Tom sade it might be the small pox or mesals so i told my wife
to give the woman some provishons and tel hur to go to the
boat and i wold put her acros in the morning so she could go
and tel the doctor on the Resirvation but when i went to the
boat i could not find hur. There was a Mr. Anes living near
us and he was going to the South Fork to a Traper Tex's
camp for some harnis and i told him to tel Tex if that woman
came to his place to send hur off for we suspected she ad beene
ware the small pox was. Tex as a wife and five children. the
woman was there all ready and Anes fetchd hur back trying
to get hur to go and live with him but she came to my camp

and asked what i wanted hur for. i told hur i did not send
for hur and told her to go away. She sade she was heavy
with child and could not walk so i told my wife to give her our
lodge [tent] and some provishons and let hur camp in the
bushes my wife and children keeping away from hur untill she
took in labor, then my wife packed her eatibles and wood to
the lodge door but did not go in. now none of us knew anything of the small pox and we suposed she was going to give
birth to a child and if there was small pox at the camp she was
clere of it as she ad beene 10 or 12 days from it then we me
and tom and Dick Jr. went to the island to kill a large buck
for mocksons and camped out one night. the next day when to
within 2 mils of home on our returne we met my wife and the

rest of my famley coming to meat us. i knew what was the mater as soone as i saw them. the indian womon was dead when we got home. when we got home we went and examined the womon and could see nothing suspisus about hur and come to the conclusion that she died in child bed. i asked my wife to take the little indian girl and wash and cleane it. she said not to do it something told hur the child wold die but at my request she took it to the house and clened it up. it played with my children for 4 days as lively as could be and that night it broke out all over with little red spots. we thought it was a rash from being washed and kept in a warme house. At this time i had the bludy flukes and was very weak from it. i had it for 5 days. when it stoped on me the child apeared to be in no misrey so when i felt better me and tom took the wagon and went up to the ranch at the elbo of the teton to kill deer for our winters meat while it was fat. i kiled 4 deer by noone the nex day but my gun shot too low witch caused me to mis severl other shots so we came downe home to resight my gun and tom borrowed Dick Juniers gun for this hunt. this was on the 13 day of December. we started up agane on the 14th my famley all feling and looking wel only my wife she complaned of drawsenes but thought nothing of it. in her state she was often so. i told Dick he could come up the 4th day from then and take a day's hunt with us. we went hunting the next morning. the dogs run some deer out and i kiled one. while i was dresing it i looked acrost the creek and saw someone with tom. thay was a long ways from me but something told me it was my son Richard and that thare was something rong at home. i started for the cabin and thay did the same. When thay saw me **Dick** sade his mother had a bad headake and wanted me at home.

he told me that himself and William was taken with a pane in the belly and my two daughters was unwel the day we left home. he had road from thair to hear in 2 hours, 20 mils and i got on the same mair and went home in les time then that. my wife was seting on the flore by the stove and my youngest daughter with her. both thair heads tyed up and sufring very mutch. my oldest daughter was in bed complaning with a pane in hur back and bely. hur looks when she answerd my questons struck my hart cold. William's legs had wekened 2 hours before i got home and he was in bed. just as i road up to the dore of the house John's legs gave way and i put him to bed. Tom and me was taken the same day and that night we did not sleep mutch, we were burning up aperntly some times and chiley at other times. we ad both lost our apitets and did not eate. i had left Dick to come down with tom and the wagon. well my wife was in labor now and i ad a hard time all alone with my famley all night and nex day about 4 o'clock my wife gave birth to a child. she had broken out all over with small red spots but after the birth of the child they allwent back on hur. i knew what the desise was as soone as i came in to the house althoe i ad never seene it before. my wife felt better and i put hur to bed. she slept well during the later part of the night and i had a hard time with all the children all night. in the morning my wife sade she wanted to get up and set by the stove. i got hur up and as i layed hur on a palit i ad fixed for hur she fainted. she shook all over and made a rumbling noyse. when she came to she sade to me: what is the mater dady? i told hur she ad fanted from weknis that was all. i was satisfide that hur hours was numberd and i spoke incorigenly to hur but my hart was ded within me. about noone she asked me to give hur some Harpers magazens and those picturs that you sent to us. she wanted to look at picturs. she looked at them and talked and asked me questons about them quite lively. it was hard work for me to answer hur without betraying my felings but i did so. the children had got quiet and some of them aslepe and i told my wife i wold go out and set fire to a brush pile to signal for tom and dick to come home. wile doing so my legs got weake and it was all i could do to get back to the cabin. i ad beene back about 10 minutes when Tom drove up with Dick taken with the small pox. Dick went out and kiled a large doe deer after i had left them and he took sick that same night. Tom was same as me with the [verolide?] i got Dick in the house and to bed and Tom went over to get Mr. Anes. Wile Tom and Anes was sounding the ice to see if a horse could cross my wife was struck with Death. she rased up and looked at me streight in the face and then she got excited and cursed Mr. Anes for bringing the Indian woman back to us and she sade she was going to die and all our children wold die and mayby i wold die. Doctor, this was the hardist blow i ad got as yet. she then layed downe and smiled at me. all at wonst she turned over to the fireplace and comenced stiring the fire. She was cold. she was laying betwixt the stove and the fireplace. i layed her downe again and put 2 pare of my socks and hur shoose on hur feet and covered hur well with blankits and a roab. she smiled and sade she felt a little warmer. i then took my gun and shot a signal for Tom and Anes. They came and I told Tom what ad hapned but did not tell Anes all. she was laying very quiet now for about 2 hours when she asked for a drink of water. i was laying downe with one of my daughters on eatch arme keeping them quiet because of the

fever. i told Anes what she wanted and he gave hur a drink and
10 minuts more she was ded. Dick turned over in bed when
he hurd the words and sade God bless my poore mother. he
then sade to me father mayby we will all die. i was talking as
incorigenly as i possably could to him when he sade well, if we
ave to die it is allright we might as well die now as some other
time. that remark was another hard blow for me. we wraped
my wife up in a blankit and Boflo roab and put hur into the
waggon bed. the next morning Mr. Anes started to the resirvation for the doctor for information how to treat the desise and
Tom went 4 mills to get John Houge. he came over and
choped wood and carid water to us he sade not to give eny
cold drinks to the children or drink eny ourselves witch advice
we followed until Mr. Anes came back from the doctor. he was
gone 2 dayes he sade the doctor sade to give them all the cold
water they wanted for it wold not hurt them. myself and Tom
did not know what to think or do about it but i sade i did not
like the idea of cold water and did not give them eny myself
nor did Tom. i ad not slept one minut since the time i got home
from the hunt. Anes after taking one night sleep came in the
house and took a change of watching with me and Tom that
was geting very low downe. i cannot describe my felings or
situation at this time i knew i must ave sleep but could not get
wile laying downe a few momants to rest my legs i saw Anes
giving the children cold water and asking them often if they
did not want to drink. i beged of him not to do so. i could not
sleep so i got up and administrad to my famley agane with
the determaton of doing alli could untili died witch i was shure
i could not more than 24 hours longer for my eyes would get
full of black spots and near blind me and death would ave been

welcome only for my children. i saw the spots go back on William and Ann Jane my oldest daughter today and was satisfide that it was the effects of cold drinks. this night about 10 0 clock i ad to lay downe exosted. night before last i took 80 drops of lodnom inside of an hour at 2 doses but it ad no efect on me. this night i felt some sines of sleep but with the sines came a heavy sweting and burning and tremors. my close and the beding was ringing wet in half an hour. when it left me i told Tom and Anes ware everything was that they might want and asked them to save some of my famley if it was posable and turned over to die.

I can not wright one hundredth part that pased thrue my mind at this time as i thought deth was on me. i sade Jinny i will soone be with you and fell asleep. Tom sade i ad beene asleep a half hour when i woke up everything was wet with preperation i was very weak. i lade for 10 or 15 minuts and saw William and Anne Jane had to be taken up to ease themselves every 5 minuts and Dick Junier very restlas. i could not bare to seeit. I got up and went to elp Tom and Anes. i saw that the spots ad gone back on Dick. my determaton was to stand by them, die with them. this was cristmas eve. Anne Jane died about 8 o clock, about the time every year i used togive them a candy puling and they menchoned about the candy puling many times while sick espeshely my son John. William died on the 25 about 9 or 10 0 clock in the evening. John and Elizabeth was doing well. they was ahead of the rest in the desise the scale was out and drying up. on the night of the 26th i changed watching with Anes. i let Anes sleep from evening until 12 0 clock. as i could not sleep until one or 2 o clock then only for one or 2 hours with swet and tremors when i wold get up. Tom was taken with dyaria 2 days ago and was to weak to get up to asist us eny more. on the 26th Dick Junier died betwixt 5 and 6 o clock in the evening. last night when i woke up the fire was out but some small coles the lamp burned downe and the dore of the cabin partly open. i was frezing aperntly. when i woke up and saw Anes lening back agenst the wall asleep it gave me a starte that i can not discribe. i woke him up then got up myself. my son John had comenced to swell agane about daylight and about 8 o clock the 27 in the morning he died. on the night of the 27 i woke up cold agene and found Anes lening aganst the bed fast asleep agane. after sleeping 5 or 6 hours the fore part of the night i got up as quick as my strngth wold let me and woke him up but it was too late. Elizabeth was over all danger but this, and she caught cold and sweled up agane and died on the 28 Dec. about 2 o clock in the morning. this was the hardist blowe of all i was taken with the bludy flucks [flux?] this night and me and Tom layed betwixt life and death for severl days. me and Tom had to beg of John Houge to stay and get us wood and water. when all my famley was all ded and buried he was determind to go when me and Tom was not able to do anything and Anes harme was sweled and sore from vaxanation. i beged of him to take 2 of my horses and sadles and go to Major Donlson and cary a letter from me asking him for some blankits and clothing so that when we got well we could change before going amongst people and probley spred the desise but Houge could not see how he could go until i ofred him $250 a day, then he could go. it took him 6 days to make the trip with 2 fat and as good bottomed mairs as is on Snake river. i ad not slept more than 2 hours at a time and that was a

misrable swet and tremors sleep for the last 13 days and i
sent to Doctor Fuler on the Resirve for something to promote
sleep. the flux ad made me wakefull agane i did not expect to
live to see Houge returne but God as spared me for some work
or other i believe and i am prepared to do it whatever it is.
Houge told along the road that only 3 of my famley was ded
what his object was i can not tell althow i wrote to Donlson
by him teling him that my famley was all ded and buried. well
when he got back the 6th day me and Tom ad got the dyria
checked some with Dovers powders and i was geting from one
to two hours sleep in twenty four. my thanks and best wishes
are due to Dr. Fuler for his advice and promptness in sending me medicen which i shall not forget.

On the 20 of febury i took a span of horses and a sled
and went to the islands on the south fork for my elth for ten
days and Tom accompaned me. . . . We got back to my cabin
and fixed things ready to move to my new place at the elbo of
the teton. i shall improve the place and live and die near my
famley but i shall not be able to do enything for a few months
for my mind is disturbed at the sights that i see around me
and the work that my famley as done wile they were liveing.
the meny little presents you ave sent to me and famley i shall
keep in memory of you and of them.

It appears that Richard Leigh did not keep a journal for
a while after this, and surely it is understandable. But more
than two years after the tragedy, under date of June 14, 1878,
there is this entry:

i got to the store cept by Mr. Johnson and famley about one
o'clock. I ad not beene there since August 1876 when i took my

famley with me for to do some trading and for a plesur trip for them. Mr. Johnson ad a baby then 12 days old. My wife Jinny nursed it a grate deel wile we were thare for its mother was sickley. he is a fine boy now and i nursed and played with him plenty this time wile thare. that night after going to bed my mind run a grate deel about my wife and that child so i could notsleep and must tell the truth i ad wet eyes that night. when i go over agane i intend to take a little pacing filley 3 years old with me for that child. i intended it for my youngest daughter Elizabeth before she died. it is out of my riley breed and very small but as pirty as can be.

Dr. Merriam had no more of the journal of Beaver Dick, but we know that he lived for twenty-one years more, that he married again, an Indian woman whose name I do not have, that there was a second family, that a daughter was already grown and married. Perhaps in this he found the work God had spared him for, as he believed; yet I have a strong feeling that the climax of his life was his gallant and stubborn struggle to save his family in those black days of December 1876. It also seems strange that he made no further mention of the child Jenny bore on her deathbed, not even a mention of its sex—but it is of course sure that it could not have survived long with no mother to nurse it.

Impossible for one of us nowadays really to visualize the whole situation in that one-room log cabin in those cold winter days nearly a hundred years ago.

The end of the story of Richard Leigh comes to us in copies of letters to the men from Pennsylvania whom he had guided on hunting trips through the years, Boies Penrose, Dr.

Josiah Curtis, and Dr. J. William White. Beaver Dick himself wrote to Boies Penrose on March 8, 1899:

> Dr: i wish you wold do what you can to elp my son Will to get along with partys or anyway to make an onist living and also my Wife to make teepys and mocksons and gloves or sowing skins and roabs. i can die happy as posable if i can rely on you in this matter. Goodby my dear frend. Bill my son will go with Hague on the sheep hunt. Dr. i ad in 1848 and 9 a brother in law by name of Henry Walls and my sister Martha Walls if you ever see or here any one of that name inquire of them and if my famley ples tell tham of me.
>
> I am the son of Richard Leigh formerly of the British Navey and grandson of James Leigh formerly colnel of the 16 lancers England. i was borne on Janury 9th in 1831 in the city of manchaster England. come with my sister to Philadelphia u.s.a. when i was 7 years old. went for the Mexcin war at close of 48 atached to E coy 1st infentry 10 months then come to rocky mountins and here i die. give my dieing respects to all my frends and acquantences to you and Mrs. Penrose God bles you all.
>
> Richard Leigh
or Beaver Dick
>
> my wife will ave the tepy made for you when you come out. Catara in throat stomach and bowels that is cause of death.
>
> Dick
>
> when you come out my wife will give you eny or all of my letters you want to rede of more.

Twelve days later he wrote another letter to Dr. Boies Penrose:

My Dear Doctor

    i am dyeny and very bad stumack bowells kidneys and piles. you wold think i was Strong to look at my hand writeny but i am as weak as water. i can notlay orset only ocasonly for 5 minuts at a time. at night the doctors gives me powders to put me to sleep or i should eve beene ded 8 or 10 days ago. my insides is clene gone. i want to let you know that my Wife will ave your lodge made on time and my son Will can show you the sheep ground and the rest of the hunting grounds on this side and Doctor i beg of you to help him to get hunting partys for him. he will not disgrace you i asure you. my wife and him will let you know when the end comes. goodby to you and Mrs. Penrose and boise, Dick and Barringer robert adams and all my frends and i should ave like to see you before i crosen the line.

    God bles you all

Richard Leigh
Beaver Dick

8

Town Life

⦃ O·M ⦄

When we had lived in the Crabtrees' commodious log cabin for three years, and my mother and my younger sister Clara had come out to live with us, we got a strong urge, Mardy and I, to build our own home. I consulted my chief in the Washington office, and he felt we could count on at least a few more years of work in or near Jackson Hole.

Coming and going so frequently on the road which led east out of the town to the headquarters of the Elk Refuge, where the Nelsons lived, we had been drawn to a certain location, the edge of the big alfalfa field owned by Mr. Miller the banker, which adjoined the Refuge boundary. Here an irrigation ditch flowed, and there were several tall cottonwood trees and many willows marching out over the fields toward Flat Creek and the main highway. Right here we wanted to build

a house, and finally Mr. Miller consented to sell a little piece
of that field.

On a wet snowy day in November, Clara and I, in number-
less trips with the old Chevrolet, made the final move. I shall
never forget driving up the muddy road just after dark with
the last load. There stood our home, with light flooding warmly
from every window, a two-story tan stucco house with English-
style high-peaked roof. As I drove in I saw the children silhouetted against the dining-room window. Inside it was warm,
dinner was cooking on the new cream enamel wood- and coal-
burning range, Mother was bustling about setting the table
in the kitchen; we had no dining room furniture as yet, and I
heard Martin and Joanne in the next room excitedly showing
Clara where they were going to put all their things in their
own room.

I walked all through the house, upstairs and down. The
furnace seemed to be working well; the water seemed to be
running in bathrooms both up and downstairs. In the big room
upstairs which was to be my study, things were piled in heaps,
but in the other two rooms up there Mother and Clara had
their beds made up for the night, and downstairs I found
Mardy making up our bed in the corner bedroom. "You know,"
I said to her, "as I drove up just now, this place looked so warm
and inviting, just like a big yellow pumpkin all lit up inside.
Maybe it's going to be all right. And maybe we'll get it paid
for some day too!"

It *was* all right, and we did get it paid for. That next summer we all went into the hills again as usual and lived through the famous Gravel Creek forest fire, which was less than a mile from our camp at Enos Lake before it was quenched by rain. And the week before Christmas we welcomed Donald, all eleven beautiful pounds of him, to our family circle.

Those years went on, filled with work, with field trips and happy homecomings to the spacious pumpkin shell. The children grew; Clara took a job at the post office and worked there for several years until she went to Alaska and found romance, a good husband, and a fine family of her own. Mother was happier in Jackson Hole than we had dared hope. "I am Grandma to the whole town," she used to say. And so she was, for ten good years.

We became so involved in the life of that little community that perhaps we gave more time to its projects than we should have. But it has always been an interesting community, like the Alaskan ones and yet different.

As I think back over the rich years in that house, there keeps coming to mind one New Year's Day, perhaps it was about 1934. We had invited a group of good friends for dinner, and it was a happy day. Late that night after they had all departed and the family was asleep, Mardy and I sat on by the last embers of the fire at the end of the long living room. "You know," she said as she gazed into the fire, "I was just thinking. That group we had here today is a good example of the variety of characters there are in Jackson Hole, and maybe it's that variety that gives this valley its own special flavor. What do you think?"

"Well, I guess you're right, come to think of it."

First of all, from their dude ranch fourteen miles up the valley at Moose had come Buster and Frances and their lively little Martha. Frances had been a dude girl from Philadelphia, product of exclusive finishing schools, who came to the valley as a guest, fell in love with the country and with a cowboy who was also a bronc rider but who had many other skills. Her family did not at first approve, so they had no money, but Buster had part of a homestead grant and here they had built up a successful dude ranch.

Another guest of ours that day was also a Philadelphian, a school friend of Frances who now owned and lived in one of the most beautiful ranches in the valley. Mardy always said it was hard for her to reconcile Jeanne's very decided Eastern accent and clothing with her tremendous enthusiasm for the West, for Jackson Hole, for cattle, for the prize bulls which she raised—but maybe it wasn't as strange as we thought. Anyway, there was no question of her great love for the valley.

The mining engineer who had built his retirement home up at Moose a couple of miles from Buster and Frances was and still is one of the most entertaining citizens of Jackson Hole. He had mined in Mexico, but the sea was always calling and he had sailed the Pacific and become an expert radio operator. He and his beautiful daughter had sailed the South Pacific for months in a small sailing ship before coming to Jackson Hole. Yet after all the years of adventure in the tropics and on all the seas and in the Orient, this world adventurer had found satisfaction and contentment in the life of this valley in the Rockies.

"And then of course," said Mardy, "there's Al. What did you think of that shooting exhibition of his?"

Our children had been given for Christmas a toy which consisted of several celluloid birds poised on a cord stretched between posts, and a BB gun with which they were supposed to knock the birds off. Buster, always as eager and interested as the children, was playing the game with them. No one was having any spectacular success, but it was fun. Suddenly Buster turned to the gray-haired trapper-wildlife photographer who was also our guest that day. "Here, Al, I bet you can shoot one from the hip, can't you?"

He thrust the little gun into Al's hand. Al said nothing, smiled in his always quiet rueful manner, quickly put the gun at his hip, fired. A little red bird fell to the floor.

"But you noticed, didn't you," I said to Mardy, "that he wouldn't try it again? Maybe you saved him by announcing just then that dinner was ready. I don't think anyone knows too much about Al's past. People here don't pry into the past and I guess it's a good thing. Buster told me that Al was in on the Klondike rush; he thinks he had a wife, who died while he was chasing the gold up there, and that he has been embittered, sort of, ever since. He's known to be a good shot, but I wonder if he could have kept on knocking off those birds!"

"But you see," went on Mardy, "what I'm thinking of—here we had a world traveler, a retired professional man who is also a ham radio operator and an architect, and two women brought up in 'high society' in the East, and a cowboy, and an old Alaska miner and trapper who is also a self-taught mechanic and photographer, and you, a biologist. And all these others so interested in Jackson Hole and the animal life here that they want you to talk to them about it all the time. Somehow all their other lives, you might say, mean less to them now than the life they find here. Pretty interesting, isn't it?"

The conversation by the fire that New Year's night had set me thinking about the composition of this valley that, thanks to the United States government, we had found ourselves living in and loving.

In the first years, 1884 and on into the early 1900's, the restless ones were seeking a home and a living, and the living in all this region in those days was cattle. So cattle was king. The first settlers in Jackson Hole were not seeking beauty for a retirement home, or mountains to climb, or slopes on which to ski. They were seeking bottomlands for raising hay, and cheap summer pastures on government land higher in the hills. The floor of this mountain valley was opened for homesteading, and all the original ranches were homesteads. Even as late as 1919, when Buster Estes came home from France, there were a few homestead entries open. The ranches in the southern end of the valley had good topsoil; those farther north had a good deal of gravel sagelands mixed with streaks of good soil. But ranching was the thing, and the town of Jackson was merely the convenience, the supply point, the meeting place.

What the ranchers wanted they pretty well got. Most of

them did not believe in wasting good money on any folderols such as better schoolhouses or higher salaries for teachers, or bridges or roads unless they were going to make it easier to get cattle to market or to the range. They could not believe that many activities besides cattle ranching could be good for the valley. Anything which threatened their summer range, their freedom, their hold on the economy and the politics of the state was automatically bad.

Perhaps none of us in those days foresaw that one day not very many years later the cattle business, while still operating and using government summer ranges, and prospering, would be far outstripped in economic value by recreation— simply allowing people to come to look at this part of the world.

Today the cattlemen have not lost anything, and perhaps we have all gained a realization that life in Jackson Hole is not one but many interests and that it is possible for all to flourish there.

But in the early 1930's we were still a tight little kingdom. There were rumors about many ranches up-country being bought by some mysterious somebody for some mysterious something, but all this, the purchasing program of John D. Rockefeller, Jr., was kept very quiet in those years. Later it would come out—as a program for adding lands to the new Grand Teton National Park (created in 1929 and including only the Tetons themselves and the lakes at their feet)—and would be the cause of years of bitter bickering. But at this time we were still wrapped up in our own affairs and all the affairs of the community.

Mardy was learning a little more about life and people. She was waging a battle, as clerk of the school board, for a new grade-school building. The trouble was, she had grown up in Alaska, where the attitude was "nothing's too good for the kids," and there had always been money for schools and for high salaries for good teachers.

The morning after the new school bond had been defeated by thirteen votes, she was ready to move back to Alaska, but she had learned a lot. She was mad at those ranchers who had come in through a blinding blizzard on that February day, in their covered horse-drawn sleighs, to defeat this proposition which they felt would cost them too much. But she had to respect them too, for they had fought honestly, had forewarned her. She was perhaps even madder at the townspeople who had said: "Oh, it will pass O.K.," and had not bestirred themselves to walk a few snowy blocks to vote.

All this I now see as part of our own growing up. I think we had been so carried away by the beauty of the valley and by our idyllic summers in the wapiti wilderness that we had not realized that the people of the valley had to think of making a living, and that in this pursuit various forces worked on them —above all, the strong persistent claims of the cattle business. It made itself felt in everything that happened in the valley. So we had our first lessons in dollars vs. aesthetics. Mardy kept saying: "It just doesn't seem right, that in such a heavenly spot there should be selfishness or discord."

We both had to learn. We also learned that if anyone were in distress these same people were the first there with help of all kinds at any sacrifice. We were learning the puzzling yet invigorating diversity among people—part of the long evolution of the human spirit. Jackson Hole was and still is a fascinating microcosm reflecting all these diversities.

9

Valley in Discord

{{ O·M }}

Our car begins to take the zigzag turns and we put it into low gear just to be sure. Glancing up the slope, we soon see a piece of the road directly above us, and we know we are approaching the top of Teton Pass. Yes, there is the dip in the ridge just ahead. We leave the hairpin turns, and glide out onto the little flat at the summit.

On every trip over "the Pass" we stop for a bit, and look. Out through the gap fringed with spruce and fir and pine we look into the misty valley far below and see the blue white-flecked mountains beyond. Beside us there is a rustic sign: "Howdy, Stranger. Yonder is Jackson Hole, the last of the Old West."

Those of us who are not strangers, those of us who live down there in the misty blue, will, if we are honest, confess to a little tightening of the throat each time this view bursts upon us. Is that slight mistiness in the scenery, or in our eyes? We don't think so much about "the last of the Old West," but those forest-clad slopes, the very air we breathe, spell HOME.

The valley of Jackson Hole lies here snugly among the mountains that rise on every side. The scenery, the game herds, the wild flowers, the entire ensemble of natural attributes has combined to produce a recreational environment that gives satisfaction and inspiration to hundreds of thousands of people each year. Yet it would seem that the sheer beauty of the place, as it might be with a beautiful woman, has actually been the cause of discord and petty quarreling to a degree almost unique. Neighbor against neighbor, group against group, the feelings have smoldered, leaping out in open conflict from time to time, the bone of contention being: What to do with this beautiful place?

We all praise the memory of that group of frontiersmen of 1870 who in the face of temptation to exploit the Yellowstone region decided to boost for a great national park, the first in the world. But their problem was simpler. They were a small group, and with just a little altruistic feeling among them they could come to a decision. In the 1940's in our valley we were dealing with a situation that had settled into a stubborn groove of tradition.

Yet altruistic impulses were felt in the Jackson Hole country, too, in earlier years. They began with explorers who saw the valley in the previous century. In 1892 Owen Wister wrote: "Of all places in the Rocky Mountains that I know, it is the most beautiful, and, as it lies too high for man to build and prosper in, its trees and waters should be kept from man's irresponsible destruction. . . ."

In 1923 there was a notable occurrence, which is commemorated by a bronze plaque at the doorway of a simple log cabin on the banks of Snake River at Moose. The plaque reads:

THE MAUDE NOBLE CABIN

This cabin, erected on its present site in 1917 by Miss Maude Noble, has been preserved and renovated to commemorate a meeting held here on the evening of July 26, 1923, at which Mr. Struthers Burt, Dr. Horace Carncross, Mr. John L. Eynon, Mr. J. R. Jones and Mr. Richard Winger, all residents of Jackson Hole, presented to Mr. Horace Albright, then Superintendent of Yellowstone National Park, a plan for setting aside a portion of Jackson Hole as a National Recreation Area for the use and enjoyment of the people of the United States. The purpose of that plan has been accomplished by the establishment and enlargement of the Grand Teton National Park.

The broad vision and patriotic foresight of those who met here that July evening in 1923 will be increasingly appreciated by our country with the passing years.

Jackson Hole Preserve, Incorporated

The words on this plaque indicate only the beginning, and the end, of a stormy period in the history of Jackson Hole, a period running from 1918 into the 1950's. The purpose of the meeting at Miss Noble's cabin in 1923 was to devise a means of saving the beauty of the valley from commercial exploitation, from the ruin of its natural beauty; an appeal to have it placed under the supervision of "some public agency." Here is a memorable example of the recognition by a very few people, for the benefit of the future, of the need for safeguarding a meaningful segment of our country from the uses of commerce.

Why the need for such concern, for such an appeal? A simple chronology of events will show, I think, what threatened the valley and what human motives were at work in its history:

The years 1918 to 1923 were trying years in Jackson Hole. In 1918 Congressman Mondell introduced a bill for the extension of Yellowstone National Park to include the northern part of Jackson Hole only. Everyone in the valley was opposed to this seemingly thoughtless dumping of a part of the valley into another already large national park. Nevertheless it was twice introduced, and twice failed. During these war years the cattlemen of the valley were able to get good prices; they had visions of expanding their herds and later securing much more of the summer range in the previously created Teton National Forest in the northern and eastern parts of the valley, which at that time had been set apart for the elk herds as the Teton State Game Preserve, under control of the Wyoming State Game Commission. In 1919 the Forest Service began curtailing some use of the ranges by cattle, for the protection of the elk, and this caused angry reactions from cattlemen. Even so, the Park Service, not the Forest Service, was the most hated government bureau. The administration of Yellowstone was suspected of wanting to "swallow up" all of Jackson Hole and do away with cattle ranching and every form of private enterprise. Thus, this early in the play, the Park Service was cast as the villain of the piece.

The tragic flu epidemic of 1918–19 was followed by a severe drought and a short hay crop, but when cattle prices began to tumble after the end of the war, the Jackson Hole ranchers held on, hoping the market would rise, hoping to use more of the valley for cattle ranching; and having had to pay high prices for hay to supplement their own short crops, they found themselves in 1920 bankrupt or heavily in debt or heavily mortgaged by the local bank.

In an attempt to remedy the situation, a few cattlemen made an effort to bring sheep into the valley. Other ranchers and most of the citizens rose in hot protest, and won out, but worry and strife now permeated the clear mountain air.

These were the local events. Added to them were more ominous threats. An engineer in Cheyenne had formed a corporation known as the Teton Irrigation Company and had filed in 1909 and in 1912 on the waters of the Gros Ventre River, the Buffalo River, and Spread Creek, the most important Snake River tributaries in the valley. They claimed the purpose of this was to "water" the beautiful sagebrush floor of the valley in front of the Tetons, Antelope Flat, which had been set aside by them under the provisions of a federal law, the Carey Act. But of course the real intention was to sell the water to Idaho farmers, and although the law required the completion of their work in five years, their privilege was extended, by succeeding

State Engineers of Wyoming, for a total of twenty-seven years.

In this same unsettled period, through connivance with some local homesteaders, an Idaho corporation known as the Osgood Land and Livestock Company secured an interest in the water-storage rights on two of the valley's lakes, Emma Matilda and Two Ocean. Two years later a citizen of Jackson Hole, in going through some records at the state capitol at Cheyenne, discovered a secret filing by the Carlisle group on the waters of Jenny and Leigh lakes, the two gems at the base of the Tetons themselves.

Here were threats to the natural condition of all the main lakes and streams of the valley, and a threat to the floor of the valley itself. By 1923 the danger seemed very real and ominous to Struthers Burt and his friends who met in Maude Noble's cabin that July evening. They knew that, inexorably, the danger would grow. The water resources of Jackson Hole would be a constant temptation to the acquisitive and the greedy. Owen Wister had been wrong. Jackson Hole did *not* lie "too high for man to build and prosper in." And it now needed to "be kept from man's irresponsible destruction." There were immediate threats to the lakes and streams.

These are the reasons for the meeting in Maude Noble's cabin, for the beginning of what was later known as "the Jackson Hole Plan." I have seen the original of a petition requesting preservation of the upper end of Jackson Hole, and on it are the signatures of men who a few years later fought bitterly against establishment of either a national park or a national monument. In 1931, as in 1923, many cattlemen and

businessmen were in favor of some kind of preservation plan
which would not jeopardize their lives and their business, and
the essential purposes of the Jackson Hole Plan were endorsed
by the Jackson Hole Cattle and Horse Association. When in
1926 John D. Rockefeller, Jr., became interested and began
purchasing ranches and other private lands in upper Jackson
Hole with the avowed purpose of later turning them over to the
federal government, he was acting on the same motives, but
in a practical way. The chronology, however, does not yet become peaceful.

The banker at Jackson was Rockefeller's agent. I talked
with him many times, but he was very secretive; in those first
days, neither the purchaser nor his plans were disclosed, and
this is understandable. I asked the banker if he thought the
people of Jackson Hole would be behind the project, whatever it

was. He assured me that they would be, and that it "would be a great thing for the valley."

What happened next I shall not attempt to explain. For some reason Rockefeller selected a new purchasing agent. And that changed the whole climate of the valley. From that moment on, the banker and all his associates, many of them cattlemen, were bitterly opposed to the Jackson Hole Plan. They now seemed to see in it the ruin of the cattle business and all freedom of enterprise in Jackson Hole. The plan did not take in the whole valley, but they felt they could not trust the forces behind it; they felt there were Park Service people who wanted everything "rim to rim."

Grand Teton National Park was established in 1929 by mere transfer of National Forest lands covering the mountains and the lakes at the western edge of the valley, which had always been federal lands. The first superintendent of the new national park met the banker on the street in Jackson and was introduced. The banker said: "Well, we fought you as long as we could. You won. Now we will cooperate."

A handsome speech, under the circumstances. One can hardly imagine any substantial number of people, in or out of Wyoming, who would now consider the creation of this park ill-advised. But Rockefeller's program of purchasing private lands in the upper and eastern parts of the valley went on, and opposition to it went on too. As the years passed, it settled into a tradition. The cattlemen became somehow convinced that all their grazing rights would be taken away; the federal government was going to gobble up everything; they had forgotten that quite recently they had petitioned that a great portion of the valley be preserved for recreation and inspiration for all people for all time. As with most feuds, this thing went beyond the state of reasoning for or against a plan; it had become a personal battle, a case of loyalty to one side or to the other. As Dick Winger, the new purchasing agent for Rockefeller, and a resident of the valley since 1913, testified at one of the several Congressional hearings held in Jackson to try to straighten out the controversy: "We don't have clean killings in Jackson Hole; we just worry each other to death!"

Soon after this I got into Dick's car one day to ride home with him. He glanced over at me with a quizzical smile: "Aren't you afraid you'll be condemned now, after being seen riding with me?"

Thus it went on. Jackson Hole might be isolated from the rest of the world in winter, but it always had two burning topics for winter conversation: the elk herd and the park. Card parties, dinner parties had their embarrassments if certain ones prominent on "the other side" were present. In some inexplicable way an atmosphere was created in which one felt inhibited from even mentioning the subject. There was no such thing as getting together and talking it over. Congress and our state officials, the federal bureaus, and all the cattle and chamber-of-commerce organizations were concerned, yet through these years it was largely a local feud, a family quarrel. At intervals new rumors drifted up and down the valley. How many more ranches had Rockefeller bought? Was it all going to be added to Yellowstone, or Grand Teton, or what were they going to do with it? Then came a day in March 1943.

I had been up the valley, tramping along the banks of the

Gros Ventre River counting dead elk, for March is the month when the weak and sick succumb. As I drove back into town I stopped my car near the post office, and I noticed "Buck," the successor to the former banker, and a real leader in the community, standing in a group of people on the sidewalk. Buck and I were working together in the Boy Scout troop in which his son and our Donald were both members, and I suddenly remembered that I must ask him about the next Court of Honor. I stepped over and began to speak, but didn't get many words said. "Boy Scouts!" he exploded. "Boy Scouts! How can we talk about Boy Scouts now? Haven't you heard what they have done? The President has put our whole valley in a park!"

Thus I received the news that Franklin Roosevelt had, by Executive Order, made a National Monument of all the Rockefeller lands and some remaining federal lands in the east and north parts of the valley. At first I too was stunned. When I came through the back door, Mardy looked up from her mixing bowl: "What's the matter?"

And when I told her, her first reaction was: "But we're in the middle of a *war!* Why do it *now?*"

So we lived through a few more years of battle over the beautiful valley. Bills were introduced in Congress to abolish the Jackson Hole National Monument; more hearings were held in Washington and in the field; the State of Wyoming even brought suit against a superintendent of the Park and Monument, since it could not sue the federal government. Signs appeared in the windows of many business houses: "We are opposed to the Jackson Hole National Monument." A large sign on the outside of one store was partly blown away by a March blizzard, leaving only the word "opposed"—which pretty well expressed the current attitude. If we of the valley, all of us, were to stop now and take a calm look back, I think we might wonder what it was all about. The ranchers of the middle and north parts of the valley had all sold because they wanted to; and yet the other ranchers clung to the idea that their lands and livelihoods were going to be snatched away.

One has to live a dreadfully long time in Jackson Hole to be considered an "Old-timer." I don't think we were considered old-timers even after thirty years of living there. But in spite of this I do think that Mardy and I sensed a bit of how the "real" old-timers, the cattlemen, the long-established townspeople, felt about this "invasion" of their own chosen valley by government, by tourists, by more and more dudes, by proposals to do this or do that with the valley. It is not easy to give up a natural pro- prietary feeling of ownership and let all the world in. How did the Indians feel at the unheralded arrival of white settlers in land that had always been theirs?

One old-timer, a woman, expressed this feeling rather well when, fourteen years after the establishment of Grand Teton National Park, the bombshell of the Jackson Hole National Monument proclamation dropped into the valley: "We GAVE them the Tetons! What *more* do they want?"

Here is the ubiquitous problem: who is "They"? Grand Teton National Park now includes the Monument lands and nearly all of the lands purchased by Rockefeller, and the noise of battle has died away. Gradually we have all learned to live with it, to recognize the good it holds, to be firm in opposing practices we think bad. We growl about some of the Park Service architecture at the headquarters at Moose, but it at least is limited to one spot. As one drives into and out of the town of Jackson, 14 miles to the south, passing through an unsightly parade of billboards that scar the charming scenery, one cannot help but breathe a sigh of gratitude after crossing the park boundary to find a quiet and serene landscape, marred only by a too-modern highway. It is our park; it is our government; we are they, and they are we. The American public decidedly will not leave this region alone, nor can we ask them to. They will be coming in increasing numbers; it is their country, too.

Now the cattlemen have their grazing rights on the national forest lands, and the right to drift their cattle across national park lands to reach these permits; people still have their homes; dudes still have their summer homes. No one, Old-timer or Newcomer, would now deny that the National Park has vitalized the economy of the valley a thousandfold. These material results are obvious. Our problem now is not the number of acres that are under state or private or federal jurisdiction, but whether or not we can keep most of these acres unspoiled by man; whether or not we can keep our souls receptive to the message of peace these unspoiled acres offer us.

Jackson Hole is not merely a sky-piercing range of mountains for tourists to aim their cameras at. It is a country with a spirit. Grand mountains, to be sure, but also lesser hills harboring on their wooded slopes the bulk of the game herds; a fringe of aspens in the foothills; the sage flats of the valley floor where in primitive times buffalo and antelope grazed; the Snake River bottoms, where white-tailed deer found congenial habitat within the memory of men still living. There is, as one of our neighbors said, "something about it." Those of us who have our homes here and are raising families can help interpret to the visitor the spirit of Jackson Hole, forged out of long controversy, tempered with our love for the valley, for "the something about it."

In our St. John's Hospital in Jackson there is a plaque honoring the parents who donated an operating room to the hospital in memory of their daughter who lost her life in the Tetons, and whose last entry in her diary that long-ago summer had been: "God Bless Wyoming and Keep it Wild."

10

Mad Hunting Days

{{ O·M }}

Ade and I had been out all day in a snowstorm, but we were not particularly tired. A car came along—three red-decorated hunters in an old sedan—friendly smiles. "Want a ride? Don't suppose you feel tired at all at the end of a hunt!"

These were local hunters, stubble-bearded, in old clothes, out for their winter's meat but enjoying every bit of the out-of-doors too.

That morning Ade and I, as we went on up a long slope to look over the country a bit, startled a herd ahead of us, streaming over a ridge. There was a dull crack from the other side of the hill. I saw some elk hesitate, then turn in our direction. Another crack. Someone over there was shooting and the elk stampeded down toward us.

I raised my gun and found the sight down. Those elk got away. Another was coming downhill. This time the sight was in place and the elk fell in an inert heap. Our hunt was over.

We walked over to the fallen animal. Then we spied another hunter coming over the ridge. "Do any good?" he hailed us quietly.

"Yeh, we got a cow. How about you?"

"Oh, I got one all right; but I'm looking for Neal. He's over here somewhere. I need some help to drag mine down."

"Which way're you going down?"

"Oh, we'll go down Wood's Canyon; our elk is on this side the ridge. But you'd do better to go down on the east side, the way yours is layin'."

He disappeared in the woods. In a few moments there was another shot. Neal had got his elk, too.

Just a friendly word in passing, there on the top of the mountain. No car hunting here. We had all climbed by our own efforts. We were all pulling our elk down through the woods by hand. And we were glad the other fellow had had success.

Are there two kinds of hunters? What makes the difference? Why is one grasping, self-centered, oblivious of courtesy? Is it a matter of background, environment? Sometimes I am moved to think so—to think that those who come from a competitive atmosphere, a dog-eat-dog life in heavily populated districts, are likely to behave true to that type in the hunting field. But then comes along a hunter from the "big city" who is a gentleman, who is capable, who has a keener appreciation of the smell of the pines and the rules of the game than many a backwoods crack-shot expert of the mountains.

Is it just a matter of circumstances? Do the same people

act differently where there is plenty of hunting room than where hunters are crowded in an impossible game-slaughter area? In other words, can the Game Commissions condition the hunting morals of the hunter by regulation of areas?

No, I don't think so. There just seem to be people, and people.

One fall many years ago Almer and I decided we'd get an elk. But an elk is a lot of meat and often a family gets tired of it before it is all used up. Too often a lot of it is wasted. "Suppose we get one together," suggested Almer. "Half an elk is enough for us."

"Good idea! Half an elk is all we need, too. What shall we get, a cow?"

"Yes, a good fat cow, I think that's the best."

So it was planned. We were to wait until the last day of the open season, to get the coldest possible weather in order to keep the meat. This was before freeze lockers and home freezers came to Jackson Hole. The trouble was, so many others would be planning the same way; the hills would no doubt be full of hunters.

But we would get out early; we'd be ahead of the others; we'd be up there before daylight. I was hoping all the others would not get the very same idea.

On that last day we were up and away long before daylight. Up Cache Creek, then a climb over the divide. Still dark. We crossed an open slope, through some trees, and on to another slope. Suddenly cracking sounds came to our ears. Still too dark to see, but surely there were some elk, and not far off. Had we overdone it? We had found elk, but could not see to shoot. But the dawn was coming—so gradually that I was not sure it would ever arrive. While we stood there in indecision we suddenly discovered that we could see our rifle barrels pretty well. The elk were still there on the slope above us; we could hear them. Maybe if we started for them we could see our sights by the time we got near enough to shoot.

It seemed then that events moved very fast. The elk had been disturbed and were moving away. We scrambled up the hill as best we could. I remember seeing elk crossing open places, headed for the heavy timber.

"I think we can try it now," Almer whispered.

The dawn must be coming fast; I could see my sights; at least I thought I could. "How about that cow right there?"

"All right."

The animals were now fleeing and we hastily opened fire. Perhaps I had overestimated the visibility. Perhaps there was still some lingering sleep in our eyes. At any rate, we fired a disgracefully large number of shots. The Indian is reputed to have remarked: "Hear one shot, he got 'em. Two shots, mebbe got 'em. Three shots, got away."

But our elk did not get away. We got our cow, and walked up to dress it out and plan for getting it home. We stood there looking at our trophy. We looked at each other. She was poor in flesh. Her teeth were worn to the gums.

"The grandmother of the elk herd," Almer muttered.

"She probably would have died this winter," I added.

"Yes, just one less for the men to drag away to the burial dump," answered Almer.

And then of course Almer began to laugh, and I soon

joined in. Here were we, the manager of the National Elk
Refuge and the government biologist, the two men in all of
Jackson Hole who should have been able to pick a good fat
cow elk, and we were going to have to drag and transport home
a bony old matriarch! Maybe it was worth it. Almer loved a
joke, whether on himself or on another—and this was something to laugh about through all the following years.

That afternoon we were back after our elk. Almer had
gone up with his saddle horse named Moose to snake the elk
down out of the hills to the road. I came along with a pick-up
truck, parked it, started to climb the hill.

I met one or two hunters on the trail. I reached the top of
the divide, came out of the woods, and over across an open
meadow below me I could see Almer and his white horse. He
was fastening a rope to the elk's neck. As I sauntered down the
open slope, a bull elk suddenly appeared out of some trees below me and to the right and began to cross the meadow. I
stopped to watch him idly, as I was of necessity no longer interested in hunting. But I was startled by scattered rifle fire.
Shots cracked out from both sides of the mountainside, and
then someone was shooting from above me, shooting over my
head at the elk below. I dropped to the ground as flat as I could,
and listened to the whine of bullets and the "crack-crack" of
rifles. I noticed that Almer, over on the other side, had dropped
from sight. The bull elk seemed to have a charmed life, but
finally he sank to the ground and the firing ceased. I rose and
looked around. I hadn't suspected that there were hunters there,
but now they popped out from all over the mountain slope

where they had been in hiding, and started to converge toward the fallen animal. But in a moment the bull was on his feet, struggling on.

Once more a fusillade from the slope; once more I flattened to the ground and listened to flying bullets. One of them evidently found the mark, for the bull was down again. Then he was on his feet, and we went through the same performance for the third time. But now the animal was finished. I have no idea how much ammunition had been expended by this little army of hunters before that lone elk was dead. We gathered about the carcass. There was an embarrassed hesitancy as the various nimrods tentatively suggested the success of their own rifles, testing out each other's attitude in the matter, each no doubt hoping the others would make no claim. Then two who were evidently partners, a little bolder and more determined than the others, brashly pulled out their knives and began dressing out the animal. No one had the nerve to object.

Almer and I quietly hauled out our own aged trophy, dutifully divided it in two parts, took it to our homes. Another hunting season was ended.

Occasionally the sagelands of the valley floor of northern Jackson Hole have been opened to hunting. With its various roadways, this area is accessible by automobile. I recall one year when elk were scarce in the hunting season. Mild weather had kept them back in the hills. But the cars were fairly swarming. I saw little of it at first hand, but heard of many incidents from this particular firing line. A little band of elk would straggle into the open territory. Immediately all hunters within reach would make a dash for the animals and start firing. As in the case of the lone bull elk on the mountain, the boldest ones, the nimble hunters, the fast runners, claimed the game. There were hot disputes, clash of tempers, ill feeling. I was told of one old man who shot an elk, but before he could reach it a younger man already had his tag on the animal.

"All right, take it!" shouted the old man, and emptied his rifle into the hind quarters of the prostrate animal.

"What luck?" I asked a returning neighbor.

"No chance!" he declared. "Why, there are five hundred cars up there, at least. If any elk do come through, it's just slaughter. None of that for me!"

Perhaps the most famous firing line was the one at Gardiner, Montana, where for many years elk would come over the National Park boundary to face a devastating rifle fire from a mass of assembled hunters. On occasion, when the smoke had cleared and the guns were silent and when each hunter had rushed out to claim his elk, it was found that there were more dead elk than there were hunters.

But we need not dwell on the situation in any one state, or any one locality. The firing line, in one form or another, threatens any place where game supply becomes large and where the hunting territory becomes unduly accessible. We are prone to blame state game authorities, or this and that federal agency, for failing to handle the matter more adequately. We get up in annual conventions and we pass resolutions censuring this or that policy.

The problem goes deeper. It threatens sport itself, as we

have known it in the past. It touches on conflicting tendencies in the outlook of man. Debase the hunting method, sportsmanship as we have learned to know it, and it will surely pass. After a season of mass slaughter of game by hunters in crowded territory, there has been public revulsion against the practice, and it is reflected in a more extensive feeling against "field sport," as we call it.

The problem lies partly in the mass production of sportsmen as well as of game. It is commercially profitable to have more and more hunters in the field. This is a strong incentive. Also, large associations of sportsmen are a powerful force in protecting the interests of sportsmen.

But the average hunter of today does not go far from the

highway; a mile or two at most. It has become a dilettante thing, to be accomplished with as little exertion as possible and in the shortest possible time. In order to obtain the necessary kill to keep the game herd within bounds, there is a tendency to open up more and more territory with roads for automobiles, to let in more and more lazy auto-hunters, to make demands for more game for still more hunters—a vicious circle. And with all this, we are reluctant to provide more game range; sometimes this is impossible anyway.

One fall I went up north of the Yellowstone to observe the hunting there. I had watched a band of elk climb a hill to get away from hunters they had seen. On the other side, more hunters. Down came the elk, angling across the slope. No, more hunters there. Back to the top again, confused, milling around. These were animals that had spent the summer in the high country, alert to every sound and scent of the wilderness. There they had some degree of self-assurance. They could cope with the dangers of the mountains. But here was something different. They were completely surrounded. Panic seized them and they started down the hill.

But by now it was nine o'clock—the Montana law permitted shooting to begin then. There had already been a distant boom of a high-caliber gun. Now the rifle fire crackled all around. The elk disappeared over the ridge. Rifles spoke over there. A few elk came back. The hillside opened up with new rifle fire. Several elk fell. Those remaining again got behind the ridge. Finally, after more sporadic firing, all the elk were down. Now they were only meat.

Out along the highway were the successful hunters, driv‹ ing home with elk carcasses lashed on their cars, filling their trucks. On the station platform at Gardiner were more carcasses, twisted and hacked and frozen into all manner of shapes, dragged over the grime of the floor, thrown about like any other freight. These were no longer the elk of the mountains, the wapiti. They were just meat.

Everywhere in the hills lie the feet and heads of slaughtered elk, the entrails and the lungs. The coyotes and the ravens flock to the feast. The Clark's nutcracker and the gray jay find the offal a godsend. The ever-cheerful chickadee flies out from the fir tree and picks daintily at the tallow.

Around the snow-driven yards in the town, along the streets and back alleys lie pieces of elk hide, mauled and chewed by dogs. In the spring the thawing snow will reveal a residue of elk hair, bones, tattered skin. Thus the wapiti, by devious routes, returns to Mother Earth.

Now the season has ended. The back roads are snowed in; the hills are deserted, and the snow lies deeper and deeper. A few crippled elk make their painful way down into the lowlands. And there is silence again in the mountains, only the coyotes cautiously sniffing around little piles of offal and heads.

The Mad Season has passed. No more red-capped hunters about the Town Square of Jackson, no more bodies and antlers giving strange contours to automobiles. The cold-storage plant begins to emerge from twenty-four-hour pandemonium to quiet and cleanly order. The town is quiet, and winter has come. The snow sifts down day after day, and bands of wapiti slip through the white world onto the upper meadows of the Elk Refuge. The whole valley is enjoying a little spell of quiet life before the skiing and all the other winter activities begin.

Of all the seasons, this is the quiet one.

But in those early years it was also my busy time. During the hunting season I followed the hunters—a scavenger. At every spot where game had been dressed out I found the evidence which was building up in my notes to a story of the condition of the wapiti—their fertility rate, their diseases, the amount of parasitic infestation, their general health. Throughout the hills I gathered samples of tissue to be sent to the laboratories for analysis. I had imposed on every good-natured friend and neighbor to aid me, and Mardy was getting used to receiving packages at the back door:

"Here's something for Olaus. He asked me to bring some of the stomach contents of my elk if I got one!"

Down in the basement at the end of the day I would be washing and tying up samples to be hung out to dry. Mardy has never let me forget her embarrassment of a day in our first winter. The big front porch of the Crabtree house, with its projecting log ends, was a fine place to hang things. One day the two most important ladies in Jackson came to call. After hastily moving a rack full of diapers from the middle of the living room, Mardy managed to entertain the ladies with tea and conversation. But as they were being ushered out the front door, one of them suddenly asked: "What is that?"—pointing to some big brown-stained cheesecloth-covered balls hanging at the corner of the porch.

"Well," said Mardy, "it's stomach contents of elk—you know, part of the study my husband is doing."

She told me she could just *feel* in their silence that they thought the whole thing was utter nonsense.

Actually, it did take a few years of living and working in Jackson Hole before people there began to see any good reason for my presence. I heard that an old-time cattleman had loudly announced in one of the local bars that "we don't need any fresh young college fella around here counting blades of grass so he can tell us what's the matter with the elk! We know what's the matter with 'em."

There were many theories. Every old-timer thought he knew. They were starving, or they needed salt, like cattle. But no one wanted the herd depleted. It was the great pride of Jacksone Hole, "the largest elk herd in the world." The cattlemen were willing to share the summer range of the federal lands with the elk. In summer, they all said, there was plenty of feed for both.

A few days after Mardy's first callers, the wife of the supervisor of Teton National Forest came to call. Snow had drifted around our front porch, so she came to the back door, and found me down on my knees over an old dishpan, washing intestinal contents through a copper screen, searching for parasites.

I could feel Mardy's consternation. She was after all still a bit new to the exigencies a biologist's wife may have to meet. But Mrs. McCain was more than equal to the occasion. "My land—don't think anything about it—I'm used to all this kind of doings. When Mac and I were first married, up in Montana, he was always bringing queer things in. I know it's all part of the work. You wouldn't chase the poor man out on the back porch in this cold, would you?"

She and Mardy went on into the living room. And I hurried my operations out of the way so that Mardy could come back and make a cup of tea for her guest.

Yes, in those days there was bounteous summer range for elk and cattle. It was after the hunting season, after the bulk of the herd had drifted down out of the deep snow country to the valley floor, that the elk fell on evil times. And my days became busier, more strenuous.

If the winter was a hard one and the elk were more concentrated on the fields of the Refuge, then we would begin to find elk lying dead or dying. I watched them as they lay. I watched them as they died. I did a postmortem examination of each one if I could. One dreadful winter, 1,175 died on the fields of the Refuge. I could not possibly examine every one, but I did examine hundreds, collected tissue and blood, recorded symptoms and evidence.

By this time I had verified my findings and my theories. Of the old-time ranchers who "knew" what was wrong with the elk, one had come closer than any other to the truth. He had said they sometimes got "willered," that is, "willowed"—they were, in some areas, out of other forage and were eating willow branches down below the tips.

I had found that the elk who died—the great proportion of them, at any rate—were dying, not of starvation or malnutrition, but of a disease, *necrotic stomatitis*, similar to the disease cattle-men call calf diphtheria. The bacillus that causes this infection is present everywhere, especially on the winter feed grounds of the Refuge, where the elk become concentrated. It needs only a lesion in the membranes of the mouth, throat, tongue, or gums to become lodged and set up its infection, and the lesions are caused by any unusually sharp awns in hay or grass, such as foxtail grass, or by sharp coarse fibers of willow or other browse too coarse to be easily chewed.

The course of the disease is similar to pneumonia. After the elk get too weak to stand or eat, they are doomed to die in about twenty-four hours.

There were other facets to this disease, of course, and other diseases and other factors, but this was the main cause of the elk problem.

After a winter of living with the wapiti through their dark days—watching them die, examining them, working in snow and blizzard and below-zero cold, trudging home across the fields night after night with cold and bloody hands and a few more unpleasant data in my notebook—you can imagine my joy at the spring release of the survivors out onto the greening hill-sides, up through the aspen groves, and on north to first verdure and new smooth red-brown coats and the endless freedom of the summer world.

Down in the valley at last men were trying to make things better for the famous elk herd. Almer and I figured out a safe carrying capacity for the winter range; a program of eradication of foxtail hay on Refuge lands was begun; a cattleman who is now the Governor of Wyoming helped us in comparative studies of food requirements of cattle and of elk; we carried on various other experiments on the Refuge. Most important, the State of Wyoming and the federal government were able to acquire more lands to be added to the Refuge so that there is more room for the elk to spread out and to seek their own natural forage. Besides all this, Almer started a program of leaving some of the cultivated hayfields uncut. The animals could then spread out and seek their own food further into the winter months.

In the big hay sheds, about 4,200 tons of hay are still stored each summer, but artificial feeding is not started until the elk have used the best of the natural grasses.

When the feeding has to start, it becomes another winter attraction of Jackson Hole, and it has been for many years. The management of the Refuge allows visitors to ride out onto the feed grounds on the big hayrack sleds loaded with bales of hay and pulled by teams of horses. Here is a new kind of hay ride for the winter visitor: out onto the fields and then in a great circle go the sleighs. With axes the men clip the bonds of the bales of hay, and toss them out, being careful that no wires go on the ground. And from all the reaches of the broad fields come the boarders to the meal, thousands of them. They know! And they welcome the presence of those other animals who bring them this bounty every day. It has always interested me, this acceptance of the horses, even of men riding horses—and the workers on the Refuge do often ride about the fields. But let a man afoot appear and the elk will stampede and run a long way.

Men and women, so long as they stay on that sleigh, may

make as much noise and commotion as they please; they may sing, they may wrestle and try to throw each other off, it makes no difference to the elk; they are intent on food, and if the sleigh stops a moment among them some of the bolder or hungrier ones will come right up and help themselves to a meal.

In the early years, whenever a bunch of us went out onto the feed ground, especially when a group went out to help make the annual count of the elk, we turned it into a real hay-ride picnic. We paid careful attention to the count—usually about 7,000 animals—as the circle was made, but going and coming was a time of joking and horseplay and singing. Perhaps the modern-day winter visitor is more sedate—I don't know; but in those years when we were more isolated from the outside world, we made our own fun and we did so with a great rugged vigor. There were those who were practical jokers and full of ideas; there were those who had stores of funny stories to tell; there were those who could sing, and those who could play a mouth organ and dance a jig; everyone contributed to the homemade fun, the fun of living in this far-off valley.

The memory of those spontaneous, unrehearsed, unplanned good times binds us proudly together in these later days. We are all grateful, perhaps a bit smug, that we lived in Jackson Hole before the world discovered it. And keeping track of what was happening with the elk herd was an important part of living in the valley in those days.

II

Wildlife in the Home

§ ℳ·ℳ §

We did not just live in Jackson Hole; we lived with a work. Olaus did not leave at 8 a.m. and return at 5 p.m. He lived with his study every hour, and, consciously or not, the family fitted into the pattern.

In our first autumn in the valley Olaus had to be away for three weeks, learning range plants and range-utilization methods at the Forest Service experiment station in Utah. At the same time Adolph was up in Glacier Park studying a certain species of mouse for his Ph.D. dissertation at the University of Michigan. He needed live mice of the same species—*Peromyscus*, the white-footed mouse—from another region, and so, before leaving for the East and school, young Billy Sheldon was live-trapping these on the Elk Refuge and bringing them in to me each day in tin cans tied to the horn of his pony's saddle. Olaus had built a wood and metal-screen cage before he left for

Utah. I was to collect the mice, and when he returned he would ship them to Adolph. I had my instructions about rolled oats, apples, and potatoes to be put in for food.

All day I kept myself busy with the two babies, trying not to feel too lonely. There was plenty to do: carrying water from the nearby irrigation ditch, washing baby clothes on a wash-board in the tin tubs on the back porch (Olaus had also built a wash bench for the two tubs before he left); keeping an eye on Martin as he played with his toys in the sand and sagebrush around the house; and in spare moments typing Olaus's report on the studies of the caribou of Alaska and Yukon Territory, a government report which would later be his doctoral thesis at the University of Michigan.

When I had tucked Martin into bed each night and given Joanne her last feeding, I was ready for some rest myself. Then the mice began.

Peromyscus are nocturnal. All day, while the noises of the household went on about them, they slept, curled in the big heap of cotton in one corner of the box. With darkness they came forth, to play, to cavort, ceaselessly jumping from one corner to another. I put the box in the kitchen and closed the door and tried to sleep. No use—the more mice Billy brought, the more decibels. How could such small creatures make so much noise? It was like a steady hailstorm. One night I remembered that nailed high to the back wall of the house, on the back porch, was a wooden box. I carried the mouse cage out and hoisted it to the top of this and went to bed, desperate for sleep. Wonderful quiet. I was just losing myself in velvety blackness when there was a loud thump, and another one, on the porch. Wearily I donned slippers and robe and went out. As I opened the door, a big black cat streaked down the steps. Of course! I had forgotten that Inez my sweet neighbor had been complaining about a cat hanging around their place.

I was quite determined to have some sleep that night and I had an inspiration. I carried the cage in and down the steps from the kitchen into the basement below. Before Olaus had gone he had stacked a good supply of cordwood there. I managed to lift the cage to the top of the neat stack and returned to bed. Five minutes later there was a roll of thunder from the basement which brought me to my feet trembling. Flashlight in hand, I went down in trepidation. The cage was still on top, but half of the wood was in a heap in the middle of the floor and the cat was clawing desperately to get back out through the crack under the tiny basement window.

Real peace came only with Olaus's return, whereupon he shipped off the mice. I was so glad to see him come back from town empty-handed. But he was laughing. "I thought I was going to have to bring those mice back to you! Butch Lloyd didn't know about sending live mice through the mail. He looked up all his books, and finally said: 'Well, they send young chicks through the mail every spring. I guess there's no reason we can't send mice!' So he took them, thank goodness!"

Olaus went on into the big living room to finish unpacking his suitcase. He lifted out a cardboard box, held it up to his ear. "What's that?" I said apprehensively.

"Oh, it's just one of those Uinta ground squirrels. It was

already hibernating and I want to sort of observe it during the winter. I thought we could keep it in that back bedroom where there's no heat, where we have things stored. I'll just transfer him to a little bigger box."

Two or three weeks later, when winter had really arrived and we were busily stoking the kitchen range, the wood-burning heater in the corner of the living room, and on most evenings the fireplace also, Olaus looked at the thermometer one evening and said: "You know, I think it's going to go to twenty below before morning. I just wonder if I shouldn't put a little something on top of that squirrel, just enough to raise the temperature a few degrees. How about this pillow?"

He picked up a round silk-covered rust-colored pillow from the couch. "That's the only decent sofa pillow we have, you know," I said.

"Yes, I know, but nothing will touch it; it will only be lying on top of the box."

In the morning Olaus said: "Guess I'll go see whether that squirrel is really still hibernating, or frozen stiff."

A moment later he returned to the kitchen, pillow in hand and a very sheepish grin on his face. There was a hole the size of a teacup in the middle of the rust-colored silk. "Gosh, Mardy, I wouldn't have believed just a pillow could raise the temperature enough to wake that critter up. I went in there and lifted the pillow off to see how the thing was, and there was no squirrel in the hay in the box; then I felt something wiggling inside the pillow in my hand!"

This incident ended as would hundreds of other similar

ones through all the ensuing years—in a gale of laughter. Since I could practically never get really angry at Olaus, and absolutely never stay angry with him, and since he was so dedicated to his work that every project or experiment he thought important was bound to go on despite anything or anybody, it was far better just to relax and take it all as it came.

One of the things which came next was elk skulls boiling on the kitchen stove. This was after we had moved to the new house; lovely clean-wood-shavings- and paint-smelling new house. I had been in town all afternoon and hurried up the front steps with thoughts of how quickly I could make a meat loaf for dinner, opened the door, was nearly knocked down by a terrific odor—indescribable. I shouted up the stairs: "What on earth happened?"

Olaus appeared at the head of the stairs. "Nothing happened. What do you mean?"

"I mean that horrible smell, of course. What is it?"

"Oh, does that smell? It's just some elk skulls I had to boil; you know, it's the only way I can get all the meat off, to make a good specimen. These are some that show the *necrotic stomatitis* in the jawbones, you know. I thought it would be a good time to do it while you were not using the stove."

"Where are the children?"

"Well, they went over to the Grants'."

"Where is your mother?"

"Oh, she's in her room. I guess she did say something about a smell."

And this was not the last time. Skulls had to be boiled. But after three or four more years Olaus called in the Nelson brothers and had a museum-garage built behind the house, and the museum room had a stove in it big enough to hold an old-fashioned wash boiler.

There were other things, just as startling if not as odoriferous. Olaus had that big room upstairs, but he didn't always confine his operations to it; things were likely to be laid down most anywhere, if he were thinking hard about some problem. More than once I went into my kitchen to mix a cake or start a meal, and was confronted with a glass vial of some kind of internal parasites of elk, in formaldehyde, sitting on the window-sill over the sink. The children, from age two on, knew all about Daddy's "smeldehyde" and that it was not for them.

Even the museum building and the study upstairs were not enough when Olaus came to the stage in the writing of the elk report where he had to compare antlers. I had learned to recognize a certain half-humorous questioning smile. "Mardy, I just don't know where I can set those things while I measure them. It's winter, you know."

"Yes, I know, and I know what you're thinking, too. The living room."

In retrospect it seems to me we barked our shins and stabbled ourselves on and fell over elk antlers for a week, but perhaps it was only a few days. By pushing the couch and all the big chairs back flat against the wall, we were able to get the antlers set up all along both sides of the room and across the hearth at the end, and Grandma and the children were warned to pick their way carefully.

It was not just because we were raising a family that I had insisted on the heaviest grade of inlaid linoleum for all the floors.

I think that almost every bird or mammal known to the valley was inside or outside our house over the years, dead or alive. One of the first things Olaus did after we moved into the new house in town was to build a roomy pen or cage, walled and roofed with chicken wire, at the back of the lot and near the willows. The first occupant I recall was a kit fox which some friend sent him from Colorado, and while we still had her someone brought in a coyote pup.

Meanwhile the children were growing; and they were Olaus's children. Martin had a pet skunk in the big cage for a while. Joanne had a baby ground squirrel in a box of cotton behind the kitchen range; she even tried to raise some baby mice she and Alma Ruth had found out on the Refuge, but that ended sadly because Donald, age two, thought they were something for him to play with.

It was not only what the children and Olaus brought in; anyone in the valley who found a crippled animal or bird, or a sick one, promptly brought it to us. One autumn I was away on a short trip to visit my family over in Okanogan. I had been back home only a few minutes and was unpacking my bag; might as well carry these clothes down to the laundry room right now. I dashed downstairs and into the laundry room, put the clothes in the hamper, heard a strange sound just behind me, and turned. There, perched on top of my drying rack, sat a very large great horned owl clicking his beak at me. I fled, and at the bottom of the stairs met Olaus: "Gee whiz, I didn't think

you'd be going downstairs so soon! Charlie Nelson found that owl by the road; one wing seemed to be injured."

After that we had a horned lark free in the house until he was able to fly, and then someone brought in a piñon jay, a species not known in Jackson Hole, and this one seemed to be injured in some way; he was let loose in the basement. But one day as I came up from the laundry I noticed him perched on one of the hundreds of elk skulls Olaus had ranged on shelves in the front part of the basement, deftly lifting the teeth out with his clever bill. I began to look around a bit; there on one end of a shelf was an open shoe box, one third full of elk teeth! The piñon jay went back to the wilds, and Olaus spent a good many hours trying to fit teeth back where they belonged.

One snowy January day we had something bigger to think about. In one of his letters to our dear friend Otto William Geist in Alaska, Olaus had casually mentioned that if it were sometime convenient he would appreciate having a skull or two of a real Eskimo dog since he had a vague idea of doing a comparative study of dogs of the North. Otto was engaged in archaeological work on St. Lawrence Island in Bering Sea, and we knew he would be handling pure strains of Eskimo dogs—Siberian huskies, as they are called. Earlier that winter of 1934 Olaus had not been too surprised, knowing Otto, to receive not two skulls but 150 (and the number grew to 956 before we were through), and one dog skin, and three fetal pups in well-packed jars of formaldehyde.

Then came the snowy January day when the expressman's truck appeared in our driveway and there was loud hammering on our back door. The expressman stood there with a big grin on his face. "Were you folks expecting some dogs? I've got 'em."

Olaus and all three children fairly catapulted out into the snow, and Grandma and I watched from the dining-room window, while two wooden crates were unloaded, and out of the crates came one brindle-brown full-grown prick-eared beauty, and one black and white, trembling, whining, and leaping in their ecstasy at being out of those crates. Fortunately they had chains, and the men soon had them secured to the corner posts of the backyard pen. I heard Olaus say: "How much do I owe you?"

"Not a thing. They came prepaid; the papers show that they

came to Seattle on a Coast Guard ship, and then prepaid from there. Didn't you know they were coming?"

No, of course not; that wasn't Otto's way of doing things. But when Olaus came back into the house he had a big smile on his face, and the first words were: "Gee whiz! I could just feel the liveness and strength in those bodies the minute I took hold of them. I haven't felt anything like that under my hands since those last days on the Koyukuk trail!"

Woman and housewife that I was, I had already been thinking of various problems entailed in this newest event, but all I said was: "What are they?"

"Oh, male and female of course! The brown one is the male, and I can see already he is an unusual dog."

He was, and we named him Ungiuk, after the beautiful Ungiuk in the team we had driven through the Koyukuk country on our honeymoon. He was smart and trainable and devoted to Olaus, and on the occasions when he managed to get loose he put every dog in the neighborhood on the run and scrambling for home and safety. And when he caught one of the neighbor's chickens he brought it carefully home and laid it at the back door for Olaus, who would then have to seek out the appropriate neighbor (that year *all* the neighbors had chickens!) and apologize and pay for the chicken.

Diomede the female was just beautiful female, that's all; and in May, of course, there were nine pups and we were in the dog business—lovely excitement for the children, mixed emotions for me. We sold and gave away five; the next winter Olaus had a team of five with Ungiuk as leader, and Martin was driving a black one hitched to his little coaster sled. But no one had properly estimated the ability of those dogs.

No chain seemed able to hold them. Sooner or later they would be loose and streaking for the nearest point of interest, usually a chicken house, or a cow or a horse in a nearby pasture. My housework was punctuated by anxious glances out the windows to see if all the dogs were where they belonged. Finally came a day when Grandma saw three of them streaking up the road, and Olaus ran, and arrived at the home of the four Nelson brothers in time to see Otto Nelson's prize black Orpingtons flying in all directions, and of course Ungiuk with his superior skill had already chosen the prize rooster. This was quite a blow. Olaus said: "We'll just have to build a dog run with such a high strong fence they *can't* get over!"

So Venice Grant's young brother Weldon came and labored for several days with heavy poles and heavy wire and heavy rocks, and Olaus had to leave on a field trip, and one evening at dusk Weldon came to the back porch and said:

"Mrs. Murie, I just finished the gate; I think everything's all done now."

"All right, Weldon, let's go take their chains off and let them have a little freedom."

This we did, and started back to the house. At the gate we stopped so Weldon could show me the good strong fastening he had devised; and out over the fence, right over my shoulder, came Sevoonga the big black-and-white pup!

Even though those dogs were kept chained, somehow they managed to slip their collars and dig out from under, jump over, or squeeze through, and off they would race on the scent of adventure. Ungiuk could be trained, but his pups seemed to have inherited more of their mother's qualities than his, and when he suddenly succumbed to quick distemper in the next winter we realized that our dog days had better come to an end.

None of this dampened the family's ardor about animal pets. There were plenty of other things easier to handle than dogs. Martin was interested in everything that walked, crawled, swam, or flew. In his room he and Olaus had built a glass-sided cage, and up in Olaus's study they had made an aquarium. One fall when Olaus came back from a field trip in Oklahoma his suitcase as usual held not only clothes. Two glass jars were lifted out while the children crowded close, wide-eyed, for Daddy always, or nearly always, brought something home. This time it was a king snake in one jar, a blue racer in another. The king snake was harmless, of course; the racer liked to bite, but his bite was not poisonous, unless it got infected. Martin already had a hog-nosed snake of which he was very fond. "All I can say," I said to Olaus that night, "is that I hope they stay in their cages; I know your interest knows no limits, and I can *stand* snakes, but you know I am not especially fond of them!"

A few afternoons later I came home from a committee meeting about the new library a few of us were trying to get started. Grandma met me with a casual statement in Norwegian: "The long one was out."

"For heaven's sake! What did you do?"

"Oh, I just picked him up and put him back."

"Well, I'm just glad it was you who found him and not I.

Did you say anything to the painter about it? I heard him say he hated snakes."

One of our good neighbors was a painter and paperhanger and was at the moment redecorating Joanne's room upstairs. I went up to Olaus's study now, having suddenly remembered that I had promised to finish typing his expense account. Beside the typewriter desk was the hot-air run from the furnace, set flush with the floor. And coiled neatly on top of it was Mr. Hog Nose. I rushed to the study window and threw it open. Down in the side yard, Martin and his friend Robert Hansen were busy building a so-called airplane out of scraps of lumber. "Martin! You come right up here and get that snake of yours!"

Behind me I heard a bang. Cleo getting down from his ladder. "Cleo, please don't quit us! I promise all the snakes will be in their cages with weights on top tomorrow!"

Winter and summer, fall and spring we had animals. I had been rather mystified about the building of the aquarium, but one winter Sunday Olaus and Martin announced that we were all going to go out to the warm springs on the Refuge and get things for it. By this time Donald was old enough to have a pair of skis too. As we set out, each of us had a small lard pail hanging from one ski pole. Through the fence we climbed, and out across the snowy fields we went, watching the elk herd as we skied, but keeping far away from it; and somehow that little expedition lives in my mind as one of the happiest times.

Beyond the Refuge headquarters, at the foot of what we called the "Little Butte," were warm springs flowing out into a pond. In contrast to the white world all around was bright green of watercress, saxifrage, and mosses. We took off our skis and crept close to the water, and there were little fishes swimming about.

Coming home across the fields was a bit slower, for each of us carried a bucket of spring water containing tiny bullheads, or snails, or aquatic plants for the aquarium. But Grandma had the kitchen fire going when we came trooping in the back door.

I got out of my ski clothes and into my housecoat, went to the kitchen and put the pot of chili on to heat, went inside and tuned in to the Telephone Hour on the radio, touched a match to the fire Olaus had laid in the fireplace earlier in the day, and sat back in the big green chair which the children called "Mommy's chair," and listened to the happy voices upstairs where they and Olaus were carefully ladling their treasures into the aquarium.

Sunday evening was "Mommy's night" at our house. The children prepared and served Sunday evening supper by the fireplace while Grandma and I listened to the music on the radio. Sometimes there was chili to warm up, but their favorite menu was "rubber sandwiches" made on the electric grill, and fruit salad. Most Sunday afternoons, as the children grew older and we were all skiing, we were out on the ski hill or up Cache Creek or out behind the Refuge. Wherever we went, it was wonderful to come home to warmth and music by the fire, and food of any kind served without my help.

12

The Gang of the Mountains

M·M

Winter was so peaceful. But spring always came, and mixed with my joy in all its fulfillments was also a little wonder about what might appear next, especially after the children were old enough to roam all over the lovely harmless countryside by themselves. Very early they began scrambling about the hillsides with Olaus in the spring, finding bird nests and learning how to band young birds. Martin had a pet raven for a long time, and he and Clara once brought home four baby magpies in a box, which for reasons I never understood were kept for a while on the top step of the stairs going down to the basement and which erupted into shrill cries every time I opened the door.

But these, too, eventually were taken outdoors and I had the feeling that the house was again clear and peaceful. Until the morning I was in our room making the bed, and threw back the dog-skin fur rug beside it. There sat the biggest, fattest toad

I had ever seen. (Years later, when I was having a routine physical examination, our doctor remarked: "You have a good strong heart." "Yes, I know that already," I answered. "I would have had heart failure long ago otherwise.")

Once more Martin was called in from the back yard. "Well, Mommy, I thought you knew I brought that toad in yesterday, and Daddy said I could leave it up there in his sink in the darkroom overnight. How could he get down here?"

How indeed! Martin and I looked at each other and as usual ended up laughing as we visualized that poor toad plopping out of the high sink onto the floor, and then plop, plop, plop, down all those stairs, and across the long living room, and into our bedroom, to find sanctuary beneath the fur rug. But he had to go outside too, and I guess that was the beginning of the toad business.

Between our driveway and the tall woven wire fence of the Elk Refuge lay a sixty-foot stretch of sand, dirt, weeds and wildflowers, and the irrigation ditch, and then the line of willows and cottonwoods just beside the fence. To the children this was "the dirt place" and here every kind of marvelous play could go on. They were fortunate, too, in having plenty of neighbors their own ages. I could nearly always count eight children out there in the dirt place. When Martin brought in the big toad, the project of the moment became a toad farm. They dug little channels from the irrigation ditch, banked them up, and then began collecting toads. Pieces of raw meat were placed in certain spots to attract flies so the toads would have something to eat, and children from all over town began bringing toads to our yard.

I suppose Olaus and I, with our own work, were vaguely conscious of all this but had not realized the stature of the project until a group of forestry officials from Utah drove up to the house one day to see Olaus on business, and when he met them at the front door they were all laughing: "Well, O.J., we thought you were supposed to be studying elk. How about this?"

Olaus must have looked mystified. "Come out here with us," they said, and led him out through the front gate and along the brown picket fence. Beyond the corner of our property there was the big rustic official sign of the National Elk Refuge, eight feet high. Halfway toward our front gate from this, stuck up into the top of the pickets, was a good-sized piece of cardboard on which was lettered in heavy black crayon: "Toad Refuge—All Toads Protected."

The Gang of the Mountains must have been born when Martin was no more than nine years old. He and his pals were already roaming the buttes, keeping animal pets in our back yard, starting a "museum." Adolph was visiting us that spring and one morning at breakfast as he listened to Martin and Charles, the doctor's son, planning an expedition for the day out to the Little Butte, he said: "You might as well start a gang; you know, give yourselves names, and call your gang something —how about "The Gang of the Mountains?"

Adolph could with only a few words fire the children's imaginations, and this suggestion was immediately adopted. So "The Gang" began, and continued on through the years until they were nearly through high school. With suggestions from Olaus and Adolph, there were always plenty of projects: at first, exploring the buttes behind the Refuge, building a tree house up there, collecting all kinds of specimens, and turning Joanne's playhouse in the back yard into a museum.

They soon saw that the girls might be of some use too, so they were, rather condescendingly, allowed to become members. They could help arrange the museum, and make lemonade and candy to be sold when, once a summer, they held a public "show" in the museum. So Joanne and Alma Ruth and Mary Lou and Peggy were given gang names too and allowed to trail along to the limit of their strength; and Donald, at first too little to go along, was nevertheless given a membership, and a name which he loved so much that we had to remember for quite a while not to call him anything but "Bluejay."

The usual summer day began with the arrival of Charles, lunch bag in hand, blue eyes sparkling with mischief and plans, straw hat stuck full of hawk and jay feathers and squirrel tails atop his yellow curls. Martin would be packing his lunch at the kitchen counter. If the girls were going along this day they would stop on the hill above the Elk Refuge buildings and Martin would give the gang call, the raven call, over and over, and soon Alma Ruth would come running to join them. As Martin once said to Adolph: "That brings 'em."

They explored every foot of the big butte behind the Refuge, and the little one beside it; they knew every cave, every ledge where ravens or hawks nested; they discovered old bear traps and old trapper cabins; they found old bison skulls and strange elk antlers and lugged them home. And they usually managed to get home before mothers began to worry. The

Gang were not always together, but they kept track of one another nearly every day. Harold and Sonny loved to fish; they were more likely to be down south of town on some of the little streams. Martin and Charles were nearly always roaming the hills, and Bobby often with them. Every so often they gathered at one house for a meeting, and it was assumed that the mother in the house would have cookies.

Much of the time they were in our yard, fussing with the museum, watching the toads, chasing the girls with garter snakes, which bothered those girls not at all. On the rare rainy days they might come to our house to work on specimens. I remember one rainy summer afternoon when Martin set up two card tables in the dining room and they were all there, with the skinning equipment, and a supply of mice someone had trapped, to have a lesson in preparing museum specimens. Martin had learned at the age of eight. I was at my desk in the bedroom. I had made filled cookies that morning. Every few moments, above the chatter of the boys, I heard the muscial "clunk" of the cookie-jar lid out in the kitchen. After a while I heard Sonny's voice: "Poor Mrs. Murie, we're eating all her cookies." But the "clunk" of the cookie jar lid continued.

Later there were more ambitious expeditions. Sometimes Olaus took all of them with him on a field trip, and he had Martin and Charles doing serious bird banding for him; they knew every hawk and raven nest in the whole area. They began going on overnight camping trips, and once all the boys camped far up on the big butte for three days. Some of the mothers worried. We had phone calls late at night: "Olaus, do you think they are all right up there? It looks like rain."

But Olaus thought the whole thing was just fine; what if it did rain on them? "They'll be all right; it's just the kind of thing boys ought to be doing, and you know, they have learned a good deal about taking care of themselves."

This was the kind of childhood which could be had in Jackson Hole. Caribou Foot, Eagle Claw, Fish Hawk, Winter Wren, Hawk Eye, Bluejay, and all the rest—for them, summer held infinite fascination under those blue Wyoming skies. On a day not long ago Joanne said to me: "You know, Mother, when I think back on those days now it seems they were just one long warm golden haze."

Sonny, who worried about my cookies, is now a politician, a member of the state legislature; Charles is a loved and successful physician in Colorado; Bobby is in the newspaper business; and Harold and Martin are both college biology professors.

Sometimes now when I am in town I go into our wonderful Teton County Library, which is a memorial to Charles's father, and I pull out the first volume of the set of Seton's *Lives of Game Animals* and there on the fly leaf is pasted a sheet which says: "Presented to Teton County Library by the Gang of the Mountains." Underneath this are the signatures of those boys who grew up in those golden days, and had museum shows for which they charged a nickel, and when they realized boyhood was over counted these collected nickels and bought a set of books for their hometown library. And went off to a war.

Jackson, Wyoming, as the Muries first saw it

The Crabtree cabin, the Muries' first home in Jackson

The "Pumpkin"--the first house the Muries built in Jackson

The new house on the ranch at Moose, Wyoming

En route to summer camp: Louis (Mrs. Murie's brother), "Grandma," Adolph Murie, and Margaret Murie astride Lady

Margaret and Olaus Murie with Martin, his three little girls, and Mildred Capron, a friend (1959)

Left: Donald Murie and Bobbie MacLeod with an elk calf, Two Ocean Lakes, Wyoming (1939) *Right:* The white mule and two of the Murie Children

Early winter on the Murie ranch

13

Whetstone Canyon

{{ O·M }}

"I do not see how anyone can live without some small place of enchantment to turn to."

So said Marjorie Rawlings, writing of her magnolia tree and the lakeside hammock of her Florida retreat.

I cannot say how many such places I have. Not, to be sure, my own legal property. Such matters transcend all strictly formal human arrangements. But, a place of enchantment? I think of several offhand. There is the spot where I stopped to rest in the wilderness of the Olympic Mountains one day— heavy forest all around, but near me a group of great maples, gracefully curved branches festooned with moss, a symphony of greens and browns in infinite variety, accented by the gold of sunlight filtering in from above. And then, when a black-tail deer came bounding through, gracefully passing under a wilderness arbor of trailing moss and young maple leaves, I was moved to do something about it. In my notebook I began: "Something beautiful happened just now."

But I got no further. How could I get a soul-filling experience like that into a small notebook that I could stuff into my pocket?

I remember too a little volcanic island in the Aleutians, a sheltered valley on the mountainside. It was a depression in the moss-covered lava rock, far above the pounding surf and shut off from the turmoil of the outer world. A group of ravens flapped by; a little winter wren broke into song; there was no other life. I think I had wearied of the buffeting of the winds of Bering Sea, the din of surf, the roaring of sea lions, the clamor of swarms of sea birds. Here was quiet. Here was the sense of shelter.

I think back to childhood days, too. One day an older girl cousin said to me: "Come, I'll show you something. A secret."

She led me down the hill in back of her house, into the woods. We walked a short distance among the trunks of elm and box elder and ash. She stopped at the foot of a tree. There was a cavity there. Over the bark and on the mold of the floor of the cavity was an infinitely smooth carpet of green moss— nothing more. "This is our secret," she said.

Childish simplicity. But for some reason the little recess in the base of that tree has remained a hallowed spot, though it was gone long ago. Did she remember in later years, she who had found it and made it a secret? If she were only here I could ask her.

In Jackson Hole, Whetstone Canyon has been such a place

for me. It is not big enough to be well known, not even big enough to be formally named, for which thank God! In fact it is a canyon in miniature, small enough to be "a place of enchantment."

I hesitate to attempt to tell of this secret lest inadequate telling destroy something that is wordless—like turning broad daylight into the charm of a twilight woods. But at any rate it is safe to speak of the spritely ouzel, the very spirit of the place. He meets you as you turn to follow the creek up into the folded hills. He bobs and curtsies on a slaty rock, regards you with frank curiosity. As you come too near, he flutters over the riffles to another rock, to teeter and bob again. He drops into the water, floats about lightly on a small eddy, even plumps to the bottom, busy about the matter of those aquatic insects. You find your way up the stream, and the steep banks become steep rocky walls, and the little sprite keeps ahead, sometimes taking a long flight with a series of notes that seem to come from the spray of the riffles, little rattling stony notes that belong between these canyon walls.

The current is swifter now, the stream winds, you jump across from rock to rock, for better going. Then, as you come around a turn in the canyon, you face the climax, a high thin waterfall.

Do not go above the waterfall. Beyond it the stream becomes ordinary. But linger. In the canyon there is much to know. It is enough just to come close to the falls for a time, to feel the spray, the cool draft from it, to press your hand against cushions of moss. Here too is the secret of the ouzel. One of these masses of moss, which seemed to be just moss, turns out to be a nest. Here the ouzels have pressed together—in a niche of the cliff, in the very spray of the water—a globular structure. The entrance is a round black hole on the side. The continual spray keeps the moss alive and the nest has become a part of the cliff. Here lives the real proprietor of Whetstone Canyon.

One day I was poking about in the talus at the foot of the banded ledges near the waterfall. Stratified rock is always intriguing. There is always the possibility of finding among those laminated petrified pages the imprints of ancient stories. I was not disappointed this time. As I cracked open a piece of shaly material, really nothing more than consolidated mud, there rolled out a fragmentary snail shell. I found many others. I found leaves, several kinds. I tried to find perfect ones, but I suppose one should not expect too much from such accidental geologic recordings. Then, as I turned over another block, I was astonished at what I saw—the clear imprint of part of a palm leaf. It was only a fragment, to be sure, but it was a palm tree, in Jackson Hole, in the Rocky Mountains.

I had come to look upon Whetsone Canyon with a feeling of ownership. Even the water ouzel, who lived there, who had first rights, had become mine.

I wonder who else has owned this place? Farther up, above the falls some distance, was an old miner's cabin, pretty well broken down now, slowly disappearing. I wondered about those miners. For a time they had lived there. Did they know about the ouzel nest? Had they found a fossil palm? Probably they had not discovered these particular "secrets" of the little canyon;

they were interested in other things. But in their day this ground was theirs.

Farther up, and high above the stream, rises a mountain mass of conglomerate and sandstone known on the maps as

Bobcat Ridge. Here too are fossil leaves. But more noticeably, among the crannies of the cliffs, live numerous marmots, or "rockchucks." On the Pacific Creek trail, years ago, I used to meet two youngsters, brother and sister, riding their ponies and followed by their dog. They lived on a ranch out near the main road and they used to ride back into the hills to Bobcat Ridge to hunt marmots. Once we rode together over part of the trail and we talked of the rockchucks and the elk and the ruffed grouse and all the other creatures which were part of the forest back here far from the roads and automobiles. We were passing through an open stand of timber when there on the green grass at one side of our trail we spotted two elk calves hiding. We reined in our horses, but just then two cow elk came up from a clump of trees. They had spied the dog and were full of fight; and the dog spied them and ran to the attack, and thereby nearly lost his life. This the elk knew how to cope with; here was another coyote. They struck at the dog savagely, their front hooves pounding the ground, missing the dog by inches. The boy and girl knew the danger instantly, spurred their horses, and screamed at the dog in terror. All this hubbub was too much for the elk—charging horses, shouting humans, barking dog—and the two mothers fled back among the trees. We too sped away as fast as possible, hoping the mothers would soon return to their young.

What had been memorable incidents in the lives of those two ranch-bred children who rode back into the hills of Whetstone for their early adventures? Now that they are grown, immersed in the practical affairs of life, do they remember?

Would they admit it? Did they too know "a place of enchant-ment"?

One spring weekend I took my own children to my Whet-stone place of enchantment, and it was like all of life—a min-gling of spiritual enrichment and earthy adventure, of aesthetics and comedy.

Joanne and Martin were in the sixth and eighth grades; Alma Ruth was in the seventh. Donald was only seven years old, but the four of them and I drove to the end of the Pacific Creek road early on a Saturday morning in late May. We then carried our sleeping bags and food up the trail about three miles. Where Whetstone Creek flows into Pacific Creek, and not too far below the big meadows which had been our first camp in Jackson Hole, we set up a little camp place for the night.

The children were full of enthusiasm. The three older ones had been studying woodcraft and first aid in Scouting and in school, and they were to write a report for their teachers on this trip. I sat on the bank under a pine tree sketching, and enjoyed watching them arrange everything. Martin and Donald were building a little fireplace of stones. They were not asking any help, but I had an idea.

"Look, Martin, there's a big flat one; let's move it over a little so the girls can use it as a kitchen table."

It was a pretty big stone, and as I was trying to ease it over another big one it slipped and fell so that its knifelike edge sliced right across my thumb, cutting a deep gash.

So there I was, the expert woodsman who had brought four youngsters on a "training trip," standing there feeling and I'm sure looking pretty foolish, with blood gushing from my thumb. I turned to my wide-eyed companions: "Well, what have you learned in First Aid?"

"Oh, we know what to do," cried Alma Ruth, first to recover her poise, "You sit down right here on this rock; here's a clean hankie; hold it around your thumb while I find something—it's good for it to bleed a little at first, you know. Come on, Joanne."

She was instantly in command of the situation. She had taken her first-aid course seriously. From the folds of her sleeping bag she produced, of all things, a roll of bandage and she and Joanne went to work on me pretty expertly while Martin got a fire going Boy Scout style, only two matches. "Your daddy should have some hot soup right away, Martin," said Alma Ruth over her shoulder.

And when the girls had finished with me, Martin produced a bandanna and Joanne a kerchief and they fashioned a sling for my arm, "so it will be supported and not throb so much," quoted Joanne with confident knowledge. "Now how do you feel, Daddy?"

"I feel all right, only pretty silly. I really didn't intend for you kids to do *all* the work on this trip!"

"Oh, that's all right; we're supposed to do it; but do you think you can go up the canyon in the morning?"

I could, and we did, and despite the throbbing in my thumb it was a day of enchantment, for it was a special pleasure to feel the enthusiasm of those children as they scrambled over boulders and waded in the water, and to hear their muted eager voices as we neared the ouzel's territory, their delight in watching the little gray water sprite, in finding for themselves his nest under the waterfall, in discovering a few fossil snails and two beautiful leaves in the loose broken shale of the canyon walls. Joanne, with her keen curiosity and sharp eyes, was in her element here. Martin was, I think, more thrilled over the glimpse we had of a little band of elk passing along, unaware of us, on the skyline above the falls. For Donald, I was sure, the chief joy was the creek itself, the rushing water, the necessity to wade in it at times. He had always been a Water Baby.

I had the feeling that for all four the chief adventure of the trip was "rescuing" me, applying first aid, doing the camp chores, being the leaders rather than followers, on this expedition. Just as well I *did* gash my thumb.

Even so, perhaps the other memories remain too. Perhaps today Alma Ruth in Kentucky and Martin in Ohio, and Joanne and Donald in Illinois, may remember the little canyon of Whetstone Creek as a "place of enchanment."

14

The Mystery of the Gros Ventre Ford

{{ O·M }}

"I'll tell you what. You come up and see me. I'd like to talk this over with you. Make it Wednesday, say two o'clock in the afternoon. Will you do that?"

He was a retired colonel who had bought a piece of land up in the Gros Ventre River basin for a summer home. He was interested in the wapiti which come into that high valley to spend the winter, and had been shocked by the number of animals that had died there. I had met the colonel first in Washington, D.C., where he had come to the office of the Fish and Wildlife Service and vehemently expressed his views on elk management in Jackson Hole.

I do not relish those emotional, heated arguments, but this

kind of thing was part of my assignment as a government employee studying the elk.

The colonel told me how to find his cabin, where to leave the main road. "You can easily ford the river at that place. It's not too deep, and there's a good bottom. We all use it."

The appointed day came and I allowed myself plenty of time for the forty-mile drive. I wondered, as I drove up the mountain road, what would be in store for me. It seemed to me that for a generation there had been nothing but controversy over this elk herd. There had been national conventions, local investigations, accusations, numerous proposals and plans. Now I was to meet once more with a man who was indignant and who could not understand why "something couldn't be done."

At that time there was only an old dirt road up the Gros Ventre River, slippery and dangerous when wet. But it was dry this autumn day and I enjoyed all the scenes I passed through. I drove over the big Gros Ventre Slide and again noted how that huge piece of mountain had slid into the deep valley and part way up the opposite hillside, where the road now runs, and the Slide Lake which had formed. Here is a powerful example of the power of earth movements. A few miles farther along I entered the spectacular Red Hills—the red formation of the Gros Ventre Range. In spring this is a startling display of bright red against the vivid green of spring growth and new leaves. Today the color scheme was tan and gold against the red, and up above in the rugged red cliffs I knew the bighorn sheep were going about their mountain living. I reveled in this red mountain valley and almost forgot the difficult mission awaiting me up the road.

I recognized the place where the colonel had told me to leave the road. Across the valley, over against the mountain, in that grove of cottonwoods I knew I would find his cabin. I turned the car down the slope and easily entered the river. Half way across the rocks began to roll and the wheels to spin, and in another moment the car came to a determined halt.

I was stuck in the middle of the river, and I was due over at the foot of that mountain shortly for another kind of ordeal. I decided to keep my appointment first. The car could wait until later, after other matters had been taken care of. I waded ashore and started across the valley afoot. I was pretty sure the sloshing water in my shoes wouldn't be noticeable by the time I got there. And it wasn't. I said nothing about being stuck in the river, for when the colonel cordially ushered me into his living room I knew I was in for a lively session.

The colonel had gathered a number of local residents, people who lived among these hills, hunted and trapped there, and had decided opinions on the elk. The air was hostile to begin with.

When we had all been seated they lost no time, and the arguments began. I quickly perceived that the talk seemed directed pretty much toward a local game warden who was evidently considered the villain. I knew that Fred was an energetic, conscientious warden who had found plenty to keep him busy in this community. The sentiments expressed could hardly be objective.

"Wait a minute," I exploded. "If this is to be a session to 'get' a certain state employee I want you to know the conference

is over right now. I will not be a party to a character assassination in this way, when the man is not here with us. If you want to talk *elk*, all right."

They looked startled and momentarily became polite, all six of them. However, I was presumed to be the elk "expert" representing the government. I, at least, was fair game, which was fair enough. I was supposed to be familiar with the elk problem. So they were soon all at me again. One of them shouted: "I'll tell *you* what's wrong with these elk!"

I knew what was coming. The popular remedy in all

cases was to feed hay. By this time I had caught the controversial spirit, and I shouted right back:

"Wait a minute. I want to tell *you* first!"

We were beginning to enjoy ourselves!

"You people, I suppose, would want to establish permanent hay-feeding grounds up here to begin with. The soil is poor. We all know that natural forage is scarce. Cattle are driven through here every spring and fall, to and from the high summer ranges beyond. Elk are expected to winter here, on poor range that is part of a cattle driveway, and you know what that means. Yet there is no other way to get those cattle through."

So far they agreed. For the time being, they were all sitting quietly, listening.

"Look at those willows out there in the creek bottoms. They're pretty well used up. Now if you start feeding hay up here you will concentrate the animals more than ever. You will build up a bigger herd, until you have many more times the elk this area can support. We have found, too, that in addition to hay the animals will go after browse. So you will lose the willows and the forest reproduction. And in spite of hay you will still have winter losses. And you can have no moose up here then, no deer. Some of these animals you speak of go on into the valley beyond, and over into Green River."

Here someone interrupted; we were entering on less tangible grounds, subject to opinions. But I persisted, warming up to my own indignation:

"People do not want to provide enough natural range for wildlife. Sportsmen demand bigger and bigger game herds but do not trouble to provide living space for them in the way nature intended. They want to simply stuff the animals with hay, the easy way—and that is supposed to settle all problems. *That's* what's the trouble with the elk!" I concluded.

This did not go over so well. They all began talking at once. No doubt about their sincerity or the eagerness of each to do the right thing for the elk. And no doubt about the right of the men who lived and hunted in the Gros Ventre hills (with some poaching on the side) to dispute the ideas of the government "expert." *They* certainly had no doubt about it, and here they had me in their own domain.

But now and then we struck common ground. Then how we joined indignantly to demolish some imaginery opponent who might think differently!

Of course we settled nothing. Not much had been settled in the previous twenty years, nor is there much prospect of public agreement in the years to come. Perhaps "what to do about the elk" is the perennial topic for our valley. But we had aired our views and we had each recognized worthy opponents.

When the colonel somewhat apologetically invited me to come again, to see him "socially" this time, and to bring my wife, I felt no need of his apology. But as I walked out through the kitchen the colonel's housekeeper turned from her work at the sink and said in a low voice: "They certainly didn't treat you fairly."

It was late afternoon as I trudged back across the flats toward the river. I was still under the spell of the stormy conference, I felt defeated, and some sort of stubborn pride had kept me from letting any of them know that I had a problem waiting for me out in the middle of the river. I had not really anticipated that the colonel would gather a roomful of people to overwhelm me. Some of them I knew were lawbreakers—at least they made their own laws about game—and I could understand why they had wanted to pounce on the reputation of Fred, a friend of mine and the most efficient game warden I had ever known. All of this was depressing. But as I approached the river I knew I now had to try for some solution to a practical, here-and-now problem. A car without traction is such a stubborn thing. What was I to do? Why hadn't I asked those fellows back there for some help?

I came out of the cottonwoods grove and stood on the riverbank. What a kaleidoscopic mental experience can be crowded into one instant! The car was not there. The river was too shallow to wash it away; I had left the keys in it; how—what—? These thoughts were but instant reactions. Across the river, up on the road, pointed toward home, sat the car. Was I awake? Was this a dream?

I fairly leapt across the river. What kind of fairy tale was I in this day? Had the whole thing been a realistic dream? But when I finally climbed in and started the car down the road, and jubilantly drove back down toward the Red Hills, it was all real enough.

To whom was I indebted for this kind act? Who had come along, back in these hills, with car, pick-up, or truck, and voluntarily undertaken to pull a strange car out of the river, leave it neatly available for travel, then gone his way? I did not know; I don't know to this day.

As I drove on toward home I pondered on the day's experiences—the discomfiture I had felt at the colonel's home; and the car stuck in the river. And in the same day the anonymous kindness that made it possible for me to be driving through the mountain dusk now toward home.

15

Love in the Wilderness

{{ O·M }}

Late one fall I had my camp near Hawk's Rest, not far from Bridger Lake, in the beautiful valley of the Upper Yellowstone River. In front of my tent was a large meadow where I picketed Lady. There was plenty of forage there for her, and Tony and the mule went free, for they would never go far from Lady.

One day I rode back into the hills as usual to observe the wapiti: what they were doing, what they were eating, where they preferred to be—all I could learn about them. It was autumn, the time of year when all life seems to be approaching maturity, when the aspens in the low country are golden and the pines and spruces higher up have matured their cones. Clark's nutcrackers flew noisily from one high ridge to another, crying raucously as is their wont when they are happy over the new pine-cone crop. A grown family of ruffed grouse walked away from me through the deep-red huckleberry bushes. For most woodfolk this is the season of harvest. Winter has already sent his warning breath, with cold frosty nights. But who cares for winter, in September?

These were the good days to be in the mountains, aside from the scientific work that had been entrusted to me. I dutifully wrote down in my notebook every fact that came to my notice, but as I look back now I realize that there was more to it than science; there were feelings and urges that enriched the experience, that made me glad I had undertaken the study.

On this particular day I had crossed the Upper Yellowstone Valley, stopped to look at a cow moose feeding on aquatic plants in Bridger Lake, then rode on up into the mountains to the west. The little white mule followed close behind all the way, like a dog. She had developed such a close attachment for Lady that she was most unhappy anywhere but at her heels and I had long ago given up trying to picket her back at camp.

I rode through the hills all day, watched several bands of wapiti, and as late afternoon came on I began to hear the bugling of the bull wapiti. They were all busy keeping together the harems of cows they had assembled. This was their mating season and they continually gave voice to the fact.

As I rode along through that sunny autumn landscape and observed all the facets of nature around me, I began to realize that all of it—the plants, the birds, the animals, all life—was looking to the future. The chickadees, the woodpeckers, all the birds I saw as I rode along, had raised their families, the youngsters were now able-bodied and on their own. Next spring they would all mate again. As I rode back toward camp I knew too that these mountain forests were full of parental love, of love for each other, of cooperation—from the plants which depended on insects to pollinate their flowers, to the many birds which depended on insects for their food while raising their young, to the wapiti, which had to have plants for food.

In my journal, as I sat on an open hillside that afternoon, I wrote what I had seen:

"I have been watching the mating performance of elk for several days. What an amazing thing for the onlooker! There is a great stir among the bulls, bugling, grunting, puffing about here and there. When there is an alarm, all flee, but the bull soon forgets danger and begins bugling again, even bugles during flight sometimes. The old herd master watches his harem. If some stray, he walks in a detour, with stately mien, and the cows meekly turn in the desired direction. He threatens them with antlers if they are too slow, and puts them on the run. Then he bellows and roars and bugles and makes a great fuss. He is full of fight and now and then threshes an innocent fir sapling with his antlers, to relieve his feelings. Coming to a boggy spot, he may set to prodding the soggy earth with his antlers and the sod goes flying into the air. He paws the ground with his hoofs, shooting clods of earth behind him. Then he lies down in the mud and perhaps still prods the earth with his antlers, wherever he can reach. The water comes into his wallow and no doubt is cooling and somewhat soothing to his fever-heated body. But he is soon on his feet again, roaring and bugling and prodding the cows around some more.

"I have spoken of the old bull. On the outskirts of the band one to four or more young bulls, two-year-olds, too young to fight the master but old enough to linger around, are watching a chance to steal a cow or two. Meek they are, these young fellows, easily put to flight at the approach of the big fellow, but ever alert. These young bucks appear more calm, are not fussing and fuming and working themselves up into an impossible state, as a rule, but I *have* seen one occasionally with mud on his side, where he had been in a wallow, and occasionally one will bugle.

"The spike bull, the youngster with his first set of antlers, mere spikes, is not in this game at all. He remains at a distance and minds his own business. He is a male, however, and the old herd master harries him off whenever he finds him in his way, and the youngster flees as a matter of course.

"What of the cows? What role do they play in all this violent lovemaking? They are mostly indifferent, so it seems. Calmly they keep on feeding, the main business of life it appears, and do not raise their heads at the terrific racket in their ears. Not interested at all; most tantalizing. If danger approaches they are alert and see it. That is something else again, and the cows are more awake than the old bull in this respect.

"What does the calf think of all this? What is all this fuss about? Probably it interests him not at all. Not given to reflection, this is all vaguely 'grown-up' business to him, if it is anything at all. He trots out of the way when antlers threaten, follows his mother when she runs before the master, and keeps on eating."

This was my record for a day of lovemaking among the wapiti.

At the end of that day I was returning by Falcon Creek to the familiar valley of the Upper Yellowstone. There across the big meadow was camp. As I began riding across the meadow, I saw in the distance a man on horseback leading two packhorses and heading in the direction of my camp. We both arrived in front of my tent at about the same moment and I recognized my visitor, a woodsman-rancher friend I had known for some time. We hailed each other in most friendly fashion and he said "Stay overnight with you?"

"Sure, Roy," I replied. "Just put your bedroll there in the tent."

We busied ourselves with horses, hobbling and picketing, making all snug about camp for the night. We cooked and ate our supper, simple fare to which we were both accustomed. Then we sat back, looking out across the open meadow. Beyond it rose the steep wall of a mountain, clothed in spruce and fir, the wilderness in all directions closing in about us as darkness fell. A bull moose walked slowly out of a patch of woods and disappeared in the dimness of a distant hollow.

Back in the tent, we lit candles and lay on our beds for a luxurious chat before turning in for the night. For a while we spoke of various things, the wildlife we both knew, our experiences in the woods. Hour after hour passed, and I began to wonder.

I don't know how the conversation turned to poetry, but Roy surprised me by quoting verse after verse of his favorite

poems. My memory of poetry was not so good. He took the lead, spoke eagerly, refreshingly. We touched on life in the wilderness, its beauties, its drawbacks, and various phases of human experience. Without great formal education, Roy had spent most of his life on the frontier, as a guide, woodsman, rancher. In his enthusiasm for poetry, he pulled some books from his pack, and the talk went on far into the night, there in the candlelight. We replenished the wood in the little stove many times. Finally there was a long pause.

"Murie, I am leaving home."

I was aghast.

"You will be hearing all about it down in the valley," he continued "I am leaving my wife."

What was there to say? What *had* I said, as I had gabbled on? Anything that had hurt?

Earnestly, at times painfully, he unfolded his story. Apparently, after all the years, there was much incompatibility. He had simply settled his affairs, taken a few belongings on two packhorses, and started out on a trail that led he knew not where. I could see that through it all he had been a gentleman, nor did he bear resentment toward his wife. "I love her," he said simply, in a voice that left me unable to make a reply.

In the morning Roy did not go on, and I did not go anywhere either. We did some chores around camp, and we talked. It was clear to me that he was hesitating to start off into a new life in the world. He was glad to be with someone, wanting to talk. So we spent the day thus and again talked into the night.

Next morning I knew Roy had reached a decision. Right after breakfast he brought his horses in from the meadow and I helped him pack them. The time had come for him to be on his way. As we shook hands he said: "Thanks for the talk. It helped."

Misty eyes in a strong man, the quivering deep voice, are unnerving. "You have this to take with you, Roy—that you have been honorable in it all!" I blurted out, and was uncertain of my own eyes and throat.

He rode away, the canvas packs on his horses swaying along the trail until they all dissolved in shadows among the spruce forests to the west. There went a human product of the wilderness—bravery, brawn a-plenty, a burly woodsman, a sensitive soul. I never saw him again.

What adventures awaited him? I never knew. But that evening, alone again in camp, I wrote in my journal:

"As I sit in my tent the wind is howling in the forest about me. When darkness fell a few hours ago, snowflakes drifted in among the tree trunks. In the meadow where the horses are grazing the grass is brown, the willows bare, and over the distant mountain crests angry clouds are gathering. Winter is surely coming to the Upper Yellowstone.

"But I find comfort in this wilderness bivouac. Supper over, I filled the stove and now have the evening for a few odd jobs, perhaps a little reading by candlelight. Tomorrow I shall break camp and may have to face a storm. But tonight in the warmth of the comfortable tent I shall not worry about that.

"Here I have had a camp in the wilderness. Adventure! But what is adventure, I wonder? Is it not often a blunder in wilderness travel that makes adventure?

"It has been my lot at times to struggle with blizzards in the far north, to travel lonely trails in Arctic mountains, or voyage by canoe through the rapids of Canadian rivers. I have had interesting experiences with the great brown bear of Alaska. But could any of these ever be equal, in adventure value, to the first camping trip as a boy in Minnesota, just a few miles out of town, with a homemade canoe and homemade tepee? Or, for that matter, the great adventure of meeting a cottontail rabbit when as a toddling youngster I had wandered out of our yard into the woods nearby?

"When I go into the wilderness today it is not the mishaps, thrilling as they may be, that I look forward to. Rather I seek the small adventures occurring from day to day. This morning, for instance, I stepped out of my tent, and in the dense fog which had settled over the meadow a great dark form loomed up, came nearer, then slowly took the shape of a big bull moose. He walked slowly by my tent and even the dim outline showed his huge massive strength, the flat palms of his antlers, and the long 'bell' hanging at his throat. I thrilled to his power and watched until he melted away in the mist.

"Then a pure white weasel came hopping up, carrying a field mouse. He dropped the mouse, directed his black beady eyes at me curiously, then as I ran toward him left his prey and scuttled over to the spring where I get my water. I picked up his mouse and examined it to see what species it was. But he did not like this. It was his mouse, and he was uneasy; I recognized his rights, dropped his mouse, and backed away. He hopped back, picked up his property, regarded me intently, and disappeared in the willows.

"Back of my camp rises a great sheer cliff. This morning a golden eagle came floating along on widespread silent pinions, soared high over the forest, and moved slowly across the face of the cliffs. Could it be that somewhere among the ledges of this rocky castle lies hidden a nest where the eagle raised his royal family last summer?

"Often from out of the forest, as I sit here writing, comes the long clear bugle note of a bull elk, while just a few moments ago, out of the darkness, came tremulous yodeling, the song of the coyote.

"These are the adventures of the wilderness, the scenes and the music which make up Nature's great mosaic. Why do we so delight in the wild creatures of the forest, some of us so passionately that it colors our whole life? Why do we love

Music, Art? Are not all akin, a part of beauty which we really do not understand?

"I know that when I have stood in Nature's domain, rapt in wonder, in the presence of some manifestation of her charm, perhaps a sunset, a mighty unfolding of mountain ranges to the horizon, or the soft hooting of an owl in the dusk, at such times I have had my greatest peace. At such times I can harbor no ill will toward my fellow man. I do not understand it. But I feel it is God-given.

"And my thoughts keep returning to Roy, to the poetry he read to me, to his sorrow. I hope he has a snug camp tonight."

16

Pioneer Poets

{{ O·M }}

After Lewis and Clark had made their famous long expedition to the Pacific and were returning home to the East, in fact when they were more than halfway there, a member of their party asked for permission to go back West. Some inner urge made him seek the freedom that could then be found in the Western wilderness. That man was John Colter. He was different.

Among all the pioneers there was diversity. So many of our movies and books play up the gun-toting, drinking, killing kind of West. In all the ages of history there has been crime; we can take our choice. I like to think of the pioneers who were also poets.

Ernest Ingersoll crossed the plains in 1877 and in 1883 wrote a book called *Knocking Round the Rockies*. When he went into the Wind River Mountains of Wyoming, he was impressed—and who wouldn't be! Here was a man who got his experience, not from a train window, but by traveling over the land. Of the Wind River Mountains he wrote: "However interesting it might prove, time forbids even to suggest all that meets the eye and is implanted in the memory while one is sitting for two or three hours on a peak of the Rocky Mountains . . ." and he speaks of his many impressions.

Then he remarks: "I can no more express with leaden type the ineffable ghost and grace of such an experience that I can weigh out to you the ozone that empurples the dust raised by the play of the antelopes in yonder amethyst valley. Moses need have chosen no particular mountain whereon to receive his inspiration. The divine heaven approaches very near all these places."

To many people, mention of the Thorofare, the Upper Yellowstone, and Big Game Ridge brings to mind precious memories. Perhaps outstanding, for some of us, is our association with wapiti in the alpine meadows. The ringing bugle call on moonlight nights in September is unforgettable. In his book Ernest Ingersoll refers to a remark of the skillful hunter Harry Young:

"Ah," says Harry, "it's finer music to listen to that old bull elk squealing up at the head of the canyon than to hear the Prussian Band."

And Ingersoll says: "It *is* better music. It arouses all the poetry of the hunter's nature—and he possesses not a little."

Osborne Russell, one of the early trappers, spent much time around 1834 in what is now Yellowstone National Park, through the Jackson Hole country and on into Utah. After his death his diary, *The Journal of a Trapper: Nine Years in the Rocky Mountains, 1834–1843*, was published. In it one can see the serious working of the mind of a trapper who got more from his wilderness experiences than the furs from his traps. I recall particularly a penetrating soliloquy composed as he looked down from the face of a mountain onto the north end of Yellowstone Lake. He mentions the herds of wapiti there, and his impressions of their wilderness environment. I like to think of this rugged trapper sitting on a mountainside, writing down his poetic thoughts about life.

One of my early friends in Jackson was Charlie Brown the blacksmith, and I was often in his shop to have my horses shod and to admire his expert work and enjoy the joking banter and tall tales that went on in that shop. But I realized years later that I had not known what was in this man's mind. After his death his wife showed me a poem he had written:

THE SHORES OF JACKSON LAKE

You may take your car and travel far,
But you will never know
Till you stand in the snow
On the shores of Jackson Lake
In the eerie light of a winter's night,
How the mountains come and go.

The coyotes play on the frozen bay,
As you listen to the breeze in the swaying trees
And the stars form a bridge to a Heavenly ridge
In the distance across the lake.

There you will know your heart can glow
To a beauty that can't be explained.
Your soul seems to open; you are close to God,
And the wonderful things he does.
No beauty elsewhere can ever compare
With the things you can see
From the shores of Jackson Lake.

I had not known that Charlie had such poetry in him; but these lines expressed, I think, the appreciation of lonely country which lay deep in the hearts of many frontiersmen. Mrs. Brown and I both felt that this verse could be dedicated to the memory of those many other pioneers who felt deeply but were not able to put their feelings into words.

One winter I was sent to attend the annual North American Wildlife Conference, which this time was being held in St. Louis. I had listened to speeches all day—bold brave words on conservation, our wild game, and the out-of-doors. But in a hotel in a big city it all had an indoor flavor for me.

That evening I visited with an old friend, Edward Preble, who had traveled much in Arctic wilderness. He made me think of Thoreau; he was the same kind of naturalist-philosopher. We talked about Hudson Bay, the caribou, life in the North. The evening passed all too quickly and when he left to catch his train I watched his taxi swirl off down the street while a loneliness came over me, as if the last link with the out-of-doors was broken.

Going back through the hotel lobby, I suddenly thought to ask for mail and was surprised when the clerk handed me a small package. In my room I hurried to open it, and found a small black notebook. It was a cheap three-ring loose-leaf type, and held a thin batch of pages. On the first page, in longhand, were the lines:

To My Friend O. J. Murie

As a lover of the wilds
I now hold you kin,
As from the surface of your paintings
I glimpsed the soul that lies within.

On the following pages was a collection of poems written in longhand by Al Austin, the trapper-photographer-mechanic who had shared that long-ago New Year's Day with us. Into my moment of boredom and loneliness the presence of a rough-clad mountaineer had come, and a quiet voice had said "Hello."

I was overwhelmed by this tribute. I no longer felt lonely. I got ready for bed, and then as I lay there in a hotel room in an Eastern city I read these verses written among Western mountains, and I pondered. The poems were written in a variety of meters, in a schoolboyish hand, spelling all awry. But they clearly expressed his attitude toward life; his understanding of his environment.

I closed the book and somewhat dreamily contemplated the field of Art today. Sentiments that were at one time respectable and worthy we have mouthed and treated with flippancy until they are virtually repudiated. More and more some art has crawled into a maze of mysterious maneuvers to find something new and unusual. Crudeness has been confused

with the picturesque. It is as if the collective Artist were doodling, and going into ecstasy over the accidental figures resulting from his erratic strokes. In all fairness, we must concede the virtue of exploration in any field. Perhaps in all this someone somewhere will make a small step forward, on which we can build.

But what of the amateurs, those earnest ones who are moved to tell their version of beauty? Shall we give them only a contemptuous glance from our stance before the Great Easel? Or can we generously credit them with a direct sincerity, perhaps a share in the profession? How about the poetic thoughts in the minds of some of the old pioneers?

One day, up in the Whetstone Creek country, Mardy and I were following the rim of a small canyon and came out on a point where we had a pleasing view of the country before us. As we stood there I noticed wapiti tracks beside me. The signs showed that a bull wapiti had come out to this point and had stood here gazing out over the valley below, just as we were doing. I recalled then what the wilderness hunter Theodore Roosevelt had once said when hunting in Two Ocean Pass: "All these elk trails have one striking peculiarity. They lead through thick timber, but every now and then send off short, well-worn branches to some cliff-edge or jutting crag, commanding a view far and wide over the country beneath. Elk love to stand on these lookout points, and scan the valleys and mountains roundabout."

Can we grant even these lowly fellow beings a vague sense of poetry, something instinctive, not well defined? Science is finding that we do have much kinship with what we call "the lower animals."

It was in these hills, on Upper Arizona Creek and Pacific Creek, that Al Austin had gone on his lone photographic expeditions. There in that hotel room in St. Louis I lay reading:

> My home is a tent, my floor is of grass.
> My grub it varies at times.
> My book is nature; each day but a page,
> My music the breeze through the pines.

Again:

> As the sun sank low in the west
> I camped at a small cold spring.
> In it water driped from a hight

With a cheerful riming ring.
That evening to write a fitting verse
In vein I tried to think,
But slept night long to its merry song,
Tinkety, Tink, Tonk, Tink.

And he wrote about other wilderness music:

The bugle-like call of an old bull elk
Is music of the sweetest strain,
The yelping note of a gray coyote
Is to me a glad refrain.

The weird call of the big gray wolf
I class with the very best
Though the creeps stampede upon one's back
It is welcomed as well as the rest.

To me, these lines show that my friend Al was a true
mountaineer, who liked and understood the music in the wilderness, real music to him, as it is to those who produce it. In
another poem he also reveals an understanding of life's problems:

Trails are crazy crooked things,
Seldom smooth and never wide.
Ways of weary wandering,
Somewhere certain to divide.
Which is right, which is rong (sic),
Which will peace and happiness bring?
Who could help one to decide?
For trails are crazy crooked things.

I was aware that in his early years Al had known sorrow; his young wife had died, and he had sought a lone life in wild country. Perhaps that can be seen in the lines:

> The trouble with the half-civilized Indian
> Is the half-savage white man.
> The Indian taught me a respect that grew
> Into deep love for the wilds.

Again:

> Did you ever suffer an attack of a wandering foot
> Caused by the Lure of that mystic unknown?
> There's no permanent cure, relief only had
> While making the wilds your home.

As a comment on this kind of life, I read his short, two-line poem which he called "A Camp and a Campfire."

> With the dreamy afterglow of evening skies
> The Ideal is more complete with coyote's cries.

Even a pioneer must anticipate an end to his travels, an end to his pioneering. I sensed this as I read the final poems in his little book. Al wrote one long poem expressing his regret at the passing of the way of life he so much admired. These are the final verses:

> Gone are the trader and old time trapper
> Who fought for their scalps day by day,
> Gone are the Reds, we have now dudes and flappers,
> Yet we are both skinned and scalped in a civilized way!

> Now, ham-strung with age, this new stuff is galling;
> I'm all ready to move camp when God names the day.

On some faraway trail when the leaves start falling,
May I die with my boots on in some old-fashioned way.

Al often referred to a song then popular, "Don't Fence
Me In." He wanted personal freedom, something people had
on the frontier along with the hardships. The little book he
sent me ended with this:

Twas good to live in Jackson Hole
Before a fence or fuss.
Equally shared by every soul,
The Golden Rule then the law for us.

With high mountain bounds on East and West
With room to go and come,
We liked our fellow-man the best
When we were scattered some.

When my old soul seeks range and rest
Beyond life's last divide,
Plant me on some strip of west
That's sunny, lone and wide.

Where the Bull Elk's bugle breaks the hush,
And Coyotes call to their kin,
Near where moose browse on willow brush,
But don't you Fence me In!

Al Austin went on his last trip back in the mountains and
made his camp. There they found him later on, in his beloved
elk hills, with his boots on. He wanted his body to enrich the
soil up there in the mountains. His thoughts, like the thoughts
of other pioneers in life, should enrich our lives, if we give
heed.

In hundreds of thousands, people now come to seek the simple beauty of unmodified scenery, giving expression to the same primal urge which brought wapiti out to the lookout points, if we understand correctly, and which brought the pioneers westward. Many of these visitors enjoy being in the midst of mountains, pine trees, riding the mountain trails, climbing the peaks. From all walks of life, from the sophistication of the great cities they come to get a touch of those moods the woodsman tried to express.

I am writing these words as I sit on the shore of a beaver pond. It is the last of May, everything coming to life in the promising spring. Before me is a patch of leaves of water lilies —they are not yet in bloom. The pond and I are surrounded by the forest, and over there to the west rise the snow-capped mountains. From here I look into the great gash between peaks which is called Death Canyon.

17

What Do You Do
All Winter?

₹ *M·M* ₹

Summer in the valley nowadays is a whirl of activity. With automobiles, more leisure, more population, and so much more publicity about the Tetons, summer is a steady stream of cars down the main highway, a colorful mass of people in the town. Fishing guides are busy on the river, climbing guides are busy in the mountains, Grand Teton National Park has colorful garlands of tourists flung along its roads, in all its visitor centers and museums, along the trails up all the canyons of the Tetons which have trails. In the hot sun under the blue blue Wyoming sky they are swimming in the lakes, floating Snake River, riding horses or hiking the trails, attending campfire programs.

Campgrounds are full, cabins are full, dude ranches and lodges are booked to overflowing. In addition to the tourists, the dudes, the visitors, are all the people young and old who make the visiting possible: the cowboys and dude wranglers and cooks and cabin girls at the dude ranches, the busboys and bellhops and waitresses and maids and mechanics at the lodges and hotels; the garage men and filling-station attendants, and all the clerks and managers in all the stores in town.

Hundreds of college students converge on Jackson Hole in June to work, and they work hard. But there are evenings, and there are days off.

Sooner or later, as summer swings sunnily and swiftly along, all of these people appear at some time or other in the streets of Jackson. And the little town is somehow ready for them. Somehow it receives and entertains two million people during a season without entirely losing its frontier look, its informal, friendly atmosphere. The chair lift on Snow King Mountain (which used to be just "Kelly's Hill") goes all day long, carrying visitors to the top for the view; the stagecoach trundles through the main streets all day long with passengers, mostly young ones, at so much per ride; the Cache Creek Posse stages a mock trial at the corner of the Town Square every evening at seven; the Pink Garter Theater produces real old-fashioned "mellerdrammer" in a wonderful Frontier Baroque Theater which used to be the Chevrolet garage. Doings which used to be a part of ordinary life are now reproduced and re-enacted for entertainment. Of course the stores, the restaurants, the hotels and motels and gift shops are all set for the tourist dollar; but here I hope they take it with a smile of gratitude.

Nature has given them the basis of their livelihood: a beautiful piece of wild country in which people love to roam, and heart-lifting scenery. And a bit of wild history which they can reenact over and over. The permanent residents of Jackson Hole are selling these things. But if they use wisdom, they are selling something which will never be exhausted.

There is bound to be a pride in living in such a place. Perhaps a touch of smugness, a proprietary feeling, is forgivable. In any case, here they choose to live, this is the resource they are selling. They would not trade place or locale with anyone, and they have a pride and a self-confidence in this. And along with it, a joy in showing their country to the visitor, a real satisfaction in helping him find the recreation he seeks, and in hearing his praise of their country.

So it is nowadays, even with the increased travel. And so it has been since the first dudes found Jackson Hole, when Jackson Hole was hard to find.

I think most people believe, and perhaps it is true in some parts, that the "natives" of any beautiful or significant summer resort rather look down on the summer visitor. One of the interesting facts about Jackson Hole is that this is not true here. I have discussed the psychology of attitude with various people in both "dude" and "native" category, and all have seen it the same way.

"Dude" was never a term of opprobrium; it simply meant a guest at a ranch or a person to be taken out hunting or fishing. It is true that in the early days most of them were from

the East, and in our valley many were from Philadelphia. Perhaps this was because the first dude ranch in Jackson Hole
was established by the beloved writer Struthers Burt, a Philadelphian.

The other interesting facet of this situation is that the
natives felt no inferiority. They were there first; they were self-
sufficient with their cattle and their land. If the dude wanted
to come and board with them and be taken riding or hunting,
the extra dollars were acceptable. The dude would be accepted
as part of the picture for a while. If he turned out to be fun and
agreeable, they would do their best for him. If he did or said
something foolish or funny, they enjoyed it; if one of their own
neighbors did something funny, they laughed at him too, but
there was no bitterness in any of this amusement. People
did not stay in this country without a sense of humor, and in
the rigorous hand-made civilization of cattle ranch life a good
joke, a funny episode, was seized on and repeated and enjoyed
—it lubricated the wheels of frontier living. The atmosphere
of early-day Jackson Hole was one of making light of hardships,
of lifting this life of hard work by joking and joshing, by kidding, with colorful phrases, by getting together now and then
to eat, and to dance all night, and have a good visit. If the dude
wanted to live this life for a while, that was fine. He added
some zest and amusement to the days, and some welcome extra
dollars to the purse.

The third point is that the dude, the one who came again
and again, liked it that way. Here he could find complete re-
laxation; who he was, how many millions he had, who his
grandfather had been, what schools he had attended, what clubs

he belonged to—none of this made any difference whatever. The folks here did not know and did not care. They looked you in the eye with absolute candor. If you fitted into their way of life, well and good. If you fell in love with the valley, came back often, perhaps bought a ranch of your own, that was all right too. You would be part of the life of the valley. You would not affect them much. They might affect you.

And they, most of them, will be here when autumn snow and cold and business pressures have sent you away from the valley.

In the height of the controversy over what to do with Jackson Hole, at a Congressional hearing in Washington, D.C., Jack Eynon, one of the pioneer cattlemen, who also "took some dudes" in summer, made the classic comment on the dude ranch. The question was: "Mr. Eynon, which do you really prefer—cattle ranching or dude ranching?"

He replied: "Dude ranching. They winter easier!"

And while they are "wintering easier," life goes on in the valley and in the town too.

In the years just before Pearl Harbor our town experienced its last idyllic winters of comparative isolation, of making our own interests and amusements without aid of television, of finding our own answers to the perennial question the summer visitor asks: "What do you do all winter?"

One mild snowy Sunday after church Edith and I, as we so often did, went for a walk and on the way back stopped, as we also so often did, at the home of Betty and Dudley. They greeted us in characteristic fashion. Betty said:

"Take off your things—I've got the coffeepot on."

Dudley said: "Betty and I have an idea."

Edith and I subsided onto a sofa. "Well, out with it!"

"We think we should start a Little Theater."

Before Edith and I had finished our coffee and Betty's delicious cinnamon rolls we were in it, no retreat. And in a few weeks the Jackson Community Theater was under way.

This kind of project, like no other activity I can think of, unless it is skiing, cuts right across social alignments, organizational rules, clubs and cliques, and brings a whole community together.

We were permitted to use the big barnlike grade-school gym. We found we had talent of every kind in our little town of some 1,400. We built our own stage, our own flats and wings, we sized and painted and made our own scenery. If I could write a play using the actual incidents of that repertory theater, it would be more exciting and amusing than any of the plays from Samuel French, Inc., which we presented.

While the cast of the first play rehearsed on stage, the work crew hammered, painted, sawed and fitted and argued, out in the auditorium. Everything had to go on at once. And every group in town was represented: Mormons and Episcopalians and Baptists; Masons and Odd Fellows and Rebekahs; bridge club and reading club and birthday club; American Legion and Auxiliary; bankers, grocerymen, plumbers, photographers, and all the rest; plus some nice boys from the CCC camp near Wilson at the foot of Teton Pass seven miles from town.

It was not surprising that Dudley, who had once been a

stage manager, should perform that function for us. It was not surprising that Betty, who had taught drama in the East, should direct plays. And I did the secretarial work, and Edith, who had a flair for interior decoration, was property and sets manager; and Dick, as actor and director of the fourth play we presented, proved brilliant in both roles.

What did surprise me was that Olaus, who up to that point in his life had seen exactly two stage performances—one of them *Ben-Hur*—not only took a lead role in the second play, *Three Live Ghosts*, but became director of the first play in our second year. But repertory theater is full of surprises and hard work, laughter, tears, and unguessed talents. Nothing surpasses the interest of watching your neighbors become new people: the telephone manager in a sophisticated love scene with the grocer's wife; the high-school basketball coach as a gigolo; the young banker as a tough cockney war hero; the pert, wise-cracking waitress in a local restaurant as a magnificently tragic old maid.

We wound up our second season gloriously with an operetta with cast of fifty. For this occasion the grocer's wife emerged as an excellent musical director, the electrician displayed a finer tenor voice than anyone had guessed he possessed, the mayor's daughter charmed us all with her soprano, the bartender's wife revealed her talent as a teacher of ballet and trained eight girls in beautiful dance scenes, and a member of the orchestra of the Cowboy Bar turned in a finished performance as the lead comedian.

I don't think the audiences ever knew about the extra scenes behind the scenes. In the midst of a love scene in the very first play, a lively rat-tat-tat of busy hammering began backstage. I got back there in time to see Dudley standing at the foot of a ladder and in an impassioned stage whisper imploring "Smitty" to come down, but "Smitty" had liquidly fortified himself for a hard evening and was determined to get the flats for the third act ready, love scene or no love scene.

On the night of the first performance of the operetta I found myself walking across the stage in a scene I did not belong in, hiding in the full skirt of my costume a fire extinguisher. Dudley snatched it from my hand as I reached the opposite wing, and soon had the fire out. We never knew how a spark had ignited a pile of scraps from the dancing costumes; the audience never knew anything had happened.

The next evening Dorothy the doctor's wife and I were in the girls' dressing room just off the wings helping the eight dancing girls change costumes. They had just finished a dance of water nymphs garbed in yards and yards of filmy pale blue gauze over pink leotards. Seven of them skipped out onto the stage as the first bars of music for the next dance sounded. The eighth girl had been basted into her costume and in places it had been sewed to her leotard. We couldn't get her out of it; the thread was tough, no one had a pair of scissors; the girl was panicky and nervous anyway, and now verging on hysteria. I looked madly about the little room. There on a high shelf was a big hunting knife which had been used by one of the pirates in *Wopping Wharf.*

I unsheathed the knife and went to work on the poor shivering girl. Her filmy blue draperies fell away from her and she fled onto the stage as the orchestra played the opening bars of the next dance for the third time, and Dorothy and I collapsed in helpless laughter stifled by mountains of pale blue gauze.

Those winters were not long enough. The day before dress rehearsal I met Dorothy coming out of the gym, her arms full of costumes: "Just let some dude ask me next summer, 'What do you do all winter?' I'll sure tell him! I've had some kind of meeting four afternoons this week, rehearsals for this thing three nights, only got to ski twice, and on Saturday I have to be gatekeeper for the high-school ski meet. I think Don and I will have to go to some city for a rest!"

But every March, no matter what else is going on, there has to be the Forty-Niner Ball.

There was one winter, not long after Adolph and my younger sister Louise were married, when they were expected for a winter stay; they had purchased a home near the foot of the ski hill and lived there when Ade's work as a government biologist permitted. On this day Olaus went to town to meet them on the mail stage. He gave Weezy a big hug, and saw the alarm on her face. And he remembered: his whiskers!

Heavy sideburns, joining with mustache and oddly trimmed mutton-chop whiskers, were that year his notion of a humorous caricature of the style of the 1840's. All the men were getting ready for the ball; we were all to be Forty-Niners. Neighbors looked curiously at each other, wondering about hirsute possibilities. There is an inherent histrionic urge, I suppose, in most of us, a pleasure in make-believe. The men I am sure enjoyed it, with a lot of good-natured kidding all round. One day as Olaus was passing a neighbor's home he heard the door open: "Take that off!" and a feminine chuckle as the door quickly closed again.

The dance used to be at the old Rainbow movie theater and dance hall. As always, we wondered where people resurrected all the old costumes, different each year, the top hats, trailing gowns, authentic trappings of a day long past. There were the inevitable Indians, bad men, gamblers, moccasined trappers. There were make-believe gambling tables, fortune-tellers, old-time dancing skits on the stage such as the "Flossie-Dossie Sextet" in which Olaus performed one year, much to my horror.

And of course some came armed with six-shooters. We had a prize waltz, and here the real Old-timers came to the fore. You can't very well simulate for the occasion the skill and native grace of the old-fashioned waltz as danced by the true old-timer who grew up with it. There were prizes for costumes, and the Grand March, and the chatter and fun of a big crowd all trying to dance when there really is not enough room.

Next day the shaggy faces were gone. Olaus admitted it was a wonderfully clean feeling.

Make-believe! The Forty-Niners! Is there a nostalgia for the bold wild days of the West? Do we hate to let it go? In our valley it is natural to remember the frontier days; they are not so far behind us here. But at the same time we are like other communities the world over. Man has discovered unheard-of mechanical power; we have the means of building a soft, easy, push-button kind of life. We stand at the threshold of a synthetic civilization, but we look back longingly to the old. What used to be a real part of life is now imitated, depicted, acted out, cherished artificially. Perhaps there is some kind of value in all this. At least it is something to think about. And the Forty-Niner Ball becomes a symbol.

18

Wings over the Snow

{{ O·M }}

December 20. This afternoon I came out of the post office with packages in my arms, and suddenly, as sometimes happens, I was taking a new look at the town. It was late afternoon and lights were on, red and green Christmas lights and bright decorations shining from the store windows on the Square. No one seems to remember why Jackson was laid out this way, with a Town Square in the middle. When we came here it was an empty, weed-grown space, but there were some good-sized cottonwoods around the edge, planted years ago, so we were told, during an upsurge of feminine power in the town, when for a year Jackson had an all-female town council and a woman mayor.

Today as I stood there just looking I remembered another snowy afternoon when Mildred Buchenroth and I had gone about as a George Washington Bicentennial Committee to solicit funds to plant and landscape the Square. Now this has been accomplished. The Square is bordered with shrubbery, green with lawn in summer and with a large natural stone in one corner, a memorial to John Colter, first white man to see the valley. This fall the final pieces were added: four tall spruces dug from the frozen ground; they will not know they have been moved until the ground thaws and they come to new life in the spring. One of them is now the town Christmas tree, its many-colored lights gleaming on the snow.

In a few days Santa will be there, and the children, singing carols. But my added pleasure today, as I stood there, was a flock of rosy pine grosbeaks fluttering and talking in their sweet notes in the planted bushes. In the middle of a busy little town, fearless and intent, they were feasting on the currant and cotoneaster berries. Bud Walters came out of his grocery store behind me:

"Pretty nice, having these little fellers right here with us, isn't it? They've been around several days now. Sure like to see 'em."

Lights from all the good neighbors' houses shone on the snowy street as I tramped home thinking of how the Square had looked, of how glad I am that it got planted, of how we live in a town that looks like an old-fashioned Christmas card.

Our house looks like a Christmas card too. School is already out, and the children and I made the fir wreath this morning and fastened it to the front door. Inside, greenery, gaudy ribbons, packages, and all sorts of good smells, and happy voices from upstairs—Joanne of course, never at a loss for words: "Martin, don't you dare open this door; this is extra-special secret!"

December 21. This morning before daylight we heard the coyote chorus out in the field. For us there was a tinge of sadness in the sound this time, for we know something they do not. The edict has come from Washington that at least ten of them are to be killed as a precaution, for it is feared that they may kill the trumpeter swans recently placed on the Elk Refuge in Flat Creek. As a matter of truth, the swans went through last winter in the presence of many coyotes. But the chorus this morning had a sad note in it for us.

Who does not respond to the brisk days of early winter? The weather was invigorating, calling us out. This morning early, a dense fog, a frosty mist hung over the land; but we wanted to do something. "How about a trip up Flat Creek, Martin? We can take the cameras along and maybe get some mountain-sheep pictures."

Martin's face beamed his pleasure even before he answered: "Sure!"

"Well, when the fog lifts, it is likely to be bright and sunny. If we are up in the canyon we will be all ready for pictures. Anyway, we are bound to see something."

Mardy and Mother were both busy with cookery. Joanne and Donald were upstairs rustling papers, wrapping gifts for their friends. But Martin and I needed to go out and do something.

Martin, at thirteen, was always ready for any expedition. With cameras, notebooks, binoculars, lunch, we were soon driving up the road leading east along the Refuge, through the foothills. We could drive to Flat Creek Canyon, northeast of town and adjoining the Refuge.

Fog hung low and dense over the land. We were passing a field when a gray figure materialized—a coyote, who appeared suddenly in our circle of vision like something thrown on a screen. He gazed at us steadfastly but when we slowed became suspicious and in seconds had faded away into the grayness as though he had not been there at all.

On this drive we would cross the Refuge, and we knew there were several thousand elk on those acres. But in the fog we could not see far. Suddenly a band of them loomed up before us, on either side. They panicked, and a line of them raced in front of the car. More and more of them poured out of the gray obscurity, became dark and clear-cut for a second, then were blotted out.

There is a coziness about fog. The wide world is shut out of the little circle of reality around you. There is only encircling grayness that conceals, encloses you in privacy, and endows the world with mystery. You wonder what may appear at any moment. Then a cow elk stands there, surprised in your own small chamber in the landscape. A tree comes forth like a figure on a print immersed in photographic developer. Rocks, limbs, bushes take form and vanish.

What is that over there? Surely eagles standing in the snow beside a carcass of a dead elk. No, they are ravens, plain to see now as they fly off into oblivion. How large everything becomes in a fog!

Then we start climbing, higher and higher, up over a hill.

The grayness is lighting, thins out, and unobtrusively we have slid out into the light, into an upper world of sunshine on snowy hills. We look back. Dense fog still hangs over the lowlands.

Presently we reached the end of our road. Cars went no farther, the snow was deeper, and here, with cameras in the packsack, notebooks in our pockets, and binoculars slung over a shoulder, we slipped into our snowshoe bindings and started for Flat Creek Canyon, less than a mile away.

We startled a band of elk and in a long line they trooped up across an open hillside. At the top of the hill they stopped to look back, the foremost ones silhouetted against the blue sky, the others huddled in a band trailing down the slope, all regarding us curiously. Martin and I stood still, absorbing one more picture: blue sky, sparkling snow, animals on the move.

In the upper limbs of a large Douglas fir were two Clark's nutcrackers busy among the cones. They would make a good photograph; I got out the Graflex and the telephoto lens; but something else attracted my attention. Not an animal; just a snow-laden limb of the tree, with drooping cones, right in front of me. I forgot the birds at the top, so engrossed was I in the beauty of that branch so close to me.

A little farther on we stopped to admire a clump of sagebrush nearly buried in snow: delicate shadows and scintillating diamonds on the white surface. I almost regretted the furrow made by our snowshoes on the pure surface. But even that was enhanced by the play of sunlight and the pale blue shadows. The little prints of a weasel, and fine traceries patterned by mice, seemed to belong there.

Across the creek, which here wound along below us, almost imprisoned by the encroaching ice, rose a steep mountainside heavily clothed in spruce and fir, a dark sunless north slope. Not here in this dark forest would we find mountain sheep. This is the domain of the pine squirrel, the owl, the marten, and the chickadee.

But on our left rose an open, somewhat shrubby slope climbing up to the base of brown and tawny cliffs. There we would expect sheep, and sure enough there they were: several ewes and a chubby-faced lamb, and a big ram ambling across the slope to join them. We had reached sheep country.

We watched this group through the glasses; admired the clean-cut uniform of grayish brown contrasting with the white rump patch, the bright stripe down the hind legs. The ram was stately with his massive sweep of horn, but there is something appealing about the simple curve of the ewe's horns too.

Up and up the slope we slogged, crossing back and forth. We encountered more sheep, finally totaling thirty-four. But they were distrustful this day and kept moving away, up into the cliffs, refusing us the pictures we had hoped to take.

I had never seen the mountain sheep in better shape. Their bellies hung low and it seemed strange that they were able to climb so well among the rocks. And the rams seemed still to be eagerly seeking the ewes. A few days before, I had been near here and had seen two rams noisily butting each other with their horns. Mating time, so close to Christmas? The wapiti had forgotten such things, for their madness comes on them in September and October. But the sheep, hardy mountaineers, seemed still to be courting in December, when winter had claimed their world. On a day like this it seemed fitting enough. They were still in a season of plenty; rabbit brush and grasses were abundant below the cliffs and the snow was not deep. The sun threw a friendly light over the brown rocks, smiling down on the sheep in their chosen home. All they need do was wander lazily over the talus slopes, nibbling the abundant forage. Enjoy it while you may, while winter is benign and the mating fever lasts!

We climbed then to a high plateau above the sheep and the cliffs. Here we found something else, large pits where wapiti had been pawing down for the grasses under the snow. They too were faring well. We saw that they had been munching mouthfuls of wheat grass, dropseed, and an occasional thistle. We came on hollows in the snow where a small herd had bedded for the night. "Look, Daddy," Martin said, pointing to a distant slope; elk trails across the snow, then in a few seconds the animals themselves, a band hurrying down across the slope. Evidently they had been in a grove of aspens and had got our scent.

The high winter pastures beckoned us on, but we must turn back. The sun was nearing the great peaks across the valley; it would soon be turning Sheep Mountain above us a vibrant pink as it sank behind the Tetons. We had started out that morning in a gray fog full of mystery; we had had bright sunlit hours with the mountain sheep; our snowshoes would leave blue shadows across the slopes as we raced the last light into the canyon. Martin's voice brought me out of my dream.

"Daddy, let's hurry. I'm starved, and Mommy promised apple dowdy for supper!"

January 21. The storm came on yesterday. By noon it was blowing and drifting and we could hardly see across the street to the Grants' house. The milkman made a delivery this morning, but I heard he did not get back to his ranch, the roads were all drifted over. The school bus did not get back to Wilson and the children stayed in Jackson all night. Mardy and Mother and I were all at the big window in the end of my study upstairs at 3:30, happy to see our three and the Grant and Steed youngsters all together, faint blurred figures hurrying through the storm.

Today the storm was still raging; the street was just a sea of swirling white, but the children wanted to go to school. Bill Grant and I assembled the nine of them on our street and broke trail for them. We took turns, one at the head of the line breaking trail, the other at the tail, with the children single-file between us, each holding the coat or belt of the one ahead. I knew that all the mothers would be watching from their windows, but they would not see us for long.

As we came back through town, it seemed like a deserted village. Bill stopped off at his grocery, but there was no one about. Allen Steed sat back there in the post office quietly reading, like a storekeeper with no goods to sell.

January 22. This noon I went out to the Elk Refuge and helped the boys load hay. Just as we finished, a bunch of elk came right up to the hay shed. Another stormy day, the air thick with snow; it is almost impossible to see where you **are** going. The elk were plastered with snow: on their faces, necks, and along their sides; surely a storm-driven lot.

We went out with our loads of hay and the elk lined out, feeding greedily, fighting over it, running here and there for a new supply. Repeatedly big bulls rose on their hind legs and boxed each other; two spikes and two cows did also. In the storm I began to see little mounds, like snowy hummocks, and realized these were dead calves, drifted over. One was lying with its head tucked in under its flank; still alive, but barely so. A forkful of hay was thrown to him, but he gave no heed. Other elk gathered about it and cheerfully ate the hay. The calf was too far gone to care; it had lost all interest and had turned its head away from all earthly things. Ravens stood in a group a little distance away. They had sized up the situation.

But winter is also something else. "Remember the day in the potholes?"

At my words a reminiscent light came into our neighbor Billy's eyes, and Edith's face beamed. That's how it was, just the thought of it made our hearts glow with the memory of that superb winter day in Upper Jackson Hole.

It was a bright crisp Sunday morning, a different kind of winter day, for winter in the valley has great variety. We had driven north from town about thirty miles, had parked our cars, climbed the bank of snow at the side, and there was a general scuffling and fussing with ski wax and bindings and poles and mittens. Then we were off.

Old Mother Earth has done well by skiers, throwing up
mountain ranges and convenient hills everywhere. And that
morning we were keenly aware of this. The retreating glacier
had left its debris of gravel in the form of rolling country here;
dips and depressions in the otherwise flat floor of the valley—
the Potholes. Gravel and boulders and sagebrush and all that
is earthy was buried deep under snow on this bright morning. Today we knew only smooth skiing, shiny slopes and
curves. There were ten of us strung out in a line, bright blue
and red and plaids against the snow. "Here we go!" shouted
Buster.

He had found a long slope into a pothole, and we watched
the slender blue ski mark moving down over the virgin snow.
One by one, in varied degrees of excellence, we followed. It was
a good run. Herring-bone back up. Down again. We tried the
high speed of the packed tracks; we slanted down over the un-
broken snow, meeting the unexpected, uncertainty. Someone
suggested we go on and look for the next pothole now, and the
slender colorful line moved on.

"Hey, wait a minute!"

It was Edith, out in front of us with her new movie camera.
And what a shot! Skiers strung out on a ridge, a little fringe
of trees, the solid black pine forest to the west, and Mount Moran
rising behind it, the great massive mountain of the range gleaming snow-white against the blue.

This was a joyous day, a buoyant landscape. We felt it
as we rode our skis through powder snow down gentle slopes.
It was suggested by the dainty patterns of jackrabbit tracks we

saw. It was reflected in the friendly chatter, the expression of our spirits, lifted by the dazzling beauty all about us.

We were no expert skiers. Ours was not the knowing, professional jargon of those masters of flight who perform miracles on a hard-packed hill. We had watched them with admiration at the ski meets which were just beginning to develop on the slope in town. We had had a little yearning and envy in our hearts. We too would like to have the skill and nerve to soar out into space from the ski jump, to turn and twist and maneuver among the flags in the slalom, or let go with abandon on the downhill.

What those able ones must enjoy! What must they experience as they take a turn at high speed, feel the bite of the ski in the snow as it swerves, feel the response of the body in its perfect balance and poise. We watch the trim figures moving on the hill in harmony with their wings of hickory, and admiration overwhelms us.

But we who do not aspire to competitions, we who may still be struggling with the snowplow or the stem turn or perhaps something a bit more ambitious, we amateurs; who shall say we do not share, and deeply, the joy of flight on skis? Do you remember the first time you rode down a slight incline and did not fall? The achievement of something new, however modest, is always memorable.

So, as we swung and dipped among the potholes on that sunny morning, with a glorious mountain range as a backdrop, it seemed we could hold no more of joy. I still recall the leap of exultation when I managed a "stem christy." I recall the thrill of speed as the wind rushed past my ears and seemed to hold me back. I remember the pulsing pleasure when I came to an unexpected bump and my skis left the snow for a moment and carried me safely on.

Modest successes, these. But I will say this for the amateur. His spirit is not jaded, his experience on skis has not become commonplace. He has attainable goals before him. His failure, his tumbles, yes, his yearning for better skill, are but wholesome spice to him. Put him in the Pothole country wherever it may be found in America, with congenial neighbors or alone, where he can feel the glow of winter sunshine reflected on snow, where he can be aware of woodland beauty, towering mountains; where he can feel the sting of driving snow and like it, or watch it fall silently among the spruces. Put him there, and if he can respond with a lift of his spirit, who shall say his joy is inferior? I salute the amateur!

As in Alaska, snowshoes were first in Jackson Hole, and when we arrived there I don't think there were many pairs of skis in the whole valley. Snowshoes, or "webs" as the Jackson Hole people call them, were the tried and true aids in getting over deep snow where a horse could not go. But by 1940 skiing had come in—or should I say, the valley had been infected by it, for many people claim it is a disease. A fairly open avenue on the forested slope south of town, called Kelly's Hill, had been "brushed out," a small ski jump had been built, a ski club organized, and we were planning a ski hut at the base of the hill. We would build it with our own hands. One resident of the valley, Fred Brown, had become an expert skier, and our children and Mardy, along with many others, were taking lessons.

One evening Martin came downstairs, ski boots in hand: "I've finished studying. You going skiing, Carc?"

"Guess not," answered Donald, who, no one knew how, had become "Carc" to his brother. "I've got a cold."

"How about you going over, Daddy?"

I looked up, startled. That hill was, in my opinion, not for amateurs, and certainly not at night. And I had planned to spend the evening by the fireplace. I looked out the window and saw the lights on the hill. It was Tuesday, one of the two nights the ski hill was lighted. Martin stood there, a quizzical smile on his face. Well— "I guess I will!"

We put my skis in the car and drove over, the first time at night for me. As for Martin, he and his pal Harold and the three older Hagen boys, and most of the other high-school students, I considered already out of my amateur class. I don't know where else in the United States high-school students have a fine ski hill just four blocks from school. The Hagens lived near the foot of the hill, and Severine, mother of four boys, was reconciled to having her house turned into a ski chalet in the winter months. (When Severine made cookies, she made double and triple batches!)

We stopped while Martin got his skis and poles from Severine's back porch. Harold and his brothers were already on the hill. In the distance the slope looked dim and I wondered if we could really see well enough to come down it. We found the tow running and saw dim shapes going up in the edge of the shadows. I joined George Lamb, another father persuaded by sons, and we started up. Other shapes were slanting downward, passing and repassing, back and forth. Soon we were up there among them.

I would not forget this experience. I had come to it so casually—a sudden response to Martin's wish. And there I stood, half way up the hill, in the center of the lighted disc. We were in a spotlight, soft, of moonlight quality. The light that in the distance had seemed so dim was ample and in some mysterious way revealed the snow so that we had no hesitation in taking off downhill. With a chuckle and a "Well, here goes nothing!" George had already left me. Around me rose a black wall of darkness. I tried to imagine the mountain rising above us into the night, the fir-clad upper slope and the snow cornice that I knew was there on the open ridge at the top. I tried to visualize Cache Creek Valley over there, with snowy peaks at its head. But it took an effort to think beyond that into the dark. So far as we were concerned, our world was this circle of light on the snow.

As for the skiers, in the misty light we hardly recognized each other. Martin and Harold had found each other and disappeared among the dream figures moving away from me; they were rapidly becoming experts; they would not waste a moment of this precious evening on the slope. Finally I forced myself out on the slope, slantwise, and found myself passing and crisscrossing with others in the dim light that cast a mellow quality over the whole scene; and mellow was the motion.

I watched a group coming down nearby, one after the

other, seemingly flowing over the rises and irregularities of the surface in an undulating procession. At the foot of the hill more people were coming out of the shadow. As I turned sharply at the end of a short run, I passed a mother and her young son climbing the hill together, herringbone fashion. There were others who came down cautiously, in short runs, experimentally —like me, pleased with a mild experience.

But the ones to watch were the boys and girls in their teens and early twenties, Fred Brown's students. They had wings on their feet. They seemed not to care whether they touched the snow or not. They came down joyously, exultantly, with shouts and laughter. They slanted back and forth across the lighted slope, with an easy lift of the shoulders at the turns. Not content with mere gliding, they would lift their skis clear of the snow in sheer delight, and I could hear the "slap-slap" as they sailed on below me.

Above me at the edge of the light, I could dimly make out the old familiar fir tree. Over against the shadowy aspens, dim shapes were going down, like ghosts, venturing out in the edge of darkness for greater thrill. They tried new routes in deeper snow, dipped into uncertain hollows. I heard Harold's laughing voice: "I might pile up. Pretty sure to!"

I saw his white-clad figure go steeply into a dip, then shoot over an abrupt rise. It seemed to leave the earth as it rose—and didn't pile up.

Beyond these skiing ghosts, in the half light, I saw streak after streak of snowy spume, like the tracks of the wind, one after another, so far over in the shadow that the figures themselves were invisible.

It haunts me like a weird ecstasy, a deep and vibrant music —that lighted snow, the laughter and joyous calling in the shadows, the deep throaty laughter. Youth on wings! Winter in Jackson Hole!

19

A Boy and His Dog

§ *M* ·*M* §

The Siberian huskies had had to go, but the children still thought about dogs—a dog. Olaus and I were so fond of the Alaska-type dog that we could hardly think of any other breed, but somewhere in the past I had visited a ranch where they were raising Norwegian elkhounds, and I had been entranced. They looked exactly like huskies but, the owner of the kennel had told me, they were the oldest-known domesticated dog in Europe, and were gentle and trainable.

Joanne, now a busy high-school freshman, found time to conduct a campaign of steady reminders. Every night when she came in from school: "Did you write about a puppy?"

She borrowed magazines from her friends, even from her piano teacher—magazines that had advertisements of kennels— and she kept the pressure on Mommy. Finally, on a January day on the way back from one of our walks out Flat Creek,

Edith and I stopped at the post office. The mail truck had just arrived from over the Pass. We stepped up to the window and Mrs. Lloyd, the chief clerk and an old friend, looked at me and then turned and called toward the back door: "Did you bring over a puppy for the Muries?"

Hobart, the young mail driver, shouted back: "Yes I did, but they can't have him; I'm going to keep him. He's the cutest pup I ever saw and he rode in my coat pocket all the way from Victor—he looked so lonesome in that big box!"

Edith called out: "Hobart, you just keep him a few minutes more; I'll have Billy come with the car and take him out to the Muries'."

Donald, who was in grade school, always got home ahead of the other two. So the great moment was his. He pulled one of the big armchairs in the living room over to face the front door, and when Martin and Joanne came in, there he sat, black eyes shining with excitement. On his lap he was holding, as Hobart had truly said, the cutest little fuzzy ball of one-month-old puppy.

Dinner hour at our house was always a great time for talk anyway, but the first days after the puppy arrived there was only one topic; what to name him. We couldn't seem to agree. At the end of a week Olaus said calmly at table one night: "Well, so far as I am concerned, the pup's name is Chimo; I'm not going to argue about a name any longer. We can't agree on a Norwegian name, and Chimo is a good Eskimo word from Hudson Bay. It means either hello or goodbye—it's a good greeting."

Chimo he was, and no dog was ever more welcome or grew to be more loved. I could write a whole book about Chimo and his adventures, but this is a story of his first field trip, in July 1941.

Two days before, Olaus and Martin had gone up Flat Creek with a load of supplies, had pioneered a route up the steep east side of Sheep Mountain, the "Sleeping Indian," and found a campsite high up there somewhere and left the tent with supplies in it. Martin could give only one day to this; he was in the business of mowing lawns that summer, to earn money for college. And Joanne was very busy with fourteen-year-old-girl affairs in the neighborhood and was going to be at the Nelsons' with Alma Ruth most of the time we were away. So this twelve-day expedition to study the food habits of mountain sheep consisted of Olaus and me and Donald, who was nine, and Chimo, six months old.

I am most relaxed when on my own two feet. The road, if it could be called such, up Flat Creek to "the countess's place," where Forney Cole was caretaker, was so narrow, so twisting, so full of big rocks that I was very glad to see the government panel truck parked safely behind Forney's barn. Forney was at home and came hurrying out of his cabin to greet us, grizzled, unkempt, his gray eyes looking through and through you. Forney had a speech impediment that made it impossible for him to pronounce "k" or "t," but we had known him a long time and understood when he said: "Chum on in, have a chuppa choffee." We knew too that when in answer to Olaus's question about leaving the truck in his barn he said: "I dunno, pad rads might jet in it," he meant "I don't know—pack rats might get in it."

Forney and his two old dogs admired Chimo, and the dogs seemed to recognize Chimo as too young to dispute their territory. Forney remarked: "Loods lide mighty fine dod. I bed he'll jus' cheep a'chomin' affer this chid here," and he put his hand on Donald's shoulder.

Not full-grown, but alive and quivering in every cell with the feeling of some new adventure, new sights and smells, Chimo jumped about and sniffed into everything while we arranged our packs. Donald had one too. "We'll start up slowly," said Olaus. "It's a warm day and it's a pretty steep way. So take it easy; we have plenty of time to get to camp before dark."

We all waved goodbye to Forney. "See you in about twelve days."

We had tried to plan this trip well, tried to figure closely the minimum amount of food we would need for the twelve days, as it would be packed up on our backs. Donald had begged to take Chimo along; they were inseparable, and Olaus thought it would be perfectly all right. "But what about food for him?"

"Oh, that will be easy," said Olaus. "I'll just wear that new Colt's Woodsman pistol Ade sent me for Christmas. You know there's a big population of ground squirrels this year."

So we started up the trail, steeply up through the pine and fir forest, then across a rockslide where coneys bleated at us but never showed themselves. Slanting up across this, we came into a more scattered forest with some white-bark pines in it, characteristic of the higher elevations, and on the edge of it, on a grassy slope full of wild geraniums and sunflowers, we sat and ate lunch and shared our sandwiches with Chimo. Then, in a nearby pine, Olaus heard a squirrel chatter. "You're not going to shoot a *tree* squirrel?"

"Well, just this one, so we'll be sure Chimo has something to eat tonight after his big climb."

Chimo sat beside Donald watching with interest as Olaus walked over to the tree. "Bang!" went the gun.

Away went the dog! Racing back down the way we had come as though shot from the gun himself, he disappeared from sight as we called and whistled frantically. "Oh well," said Olaus. "Let's finish lunch; he won't stay away long; he'll be back by the time we finish."

But he was not. No calls or whistles brought him. Olaus left his pack and went back down the mountain. Donald and I waited and watched, and while we waited Donald suddenly found an explanation. "You remember, Mommy, on the Fourth of July when we had all the fireworks in our yard with all the neighbors, and nobody thought about Chimo, and then Mac Haines found him all curled up and shivering behind the door in the front vestibule? I bet Chimo got so scared of that noise he's always going to be afraid of anything like it."

We waited for another half hour, and saw Olaus coming up the slope, alone. Three solemn-faced people shouldered their packs. "I still think he will come back," said Olaus. "But anyway we have to get this stuff up to camp and get settled before dark. Then if he isn't back by daylight, I'll have to go all the way back down and find him. I guess we've got a gun-shy dog. Don't see how I'm going to keep him fed if he is going to leave the country every time I shoot."

The morning had been sunny in every way, and we tingled with the joy of being out in the hills again. The afternoon was still sunny, and hot, but darker somehow. The gay mountain meadows were shadowed over with the worrisome thought of what might have happened to the missing member of our party. If he went back to Forney's he would be all right, but would he go there?

The way became steeper and muscles became tired, and our progress was plodding and slow and dusk was falling and we had not yet reached the little nook of forest and meadow where Olaus and Martin had made our camp. Finally Olaus turned and looked at us. Donald had not complained, but he was lagging behind and kept looking back down over the slopes below. Never loquacious, he had hardly spoken as we toiled upward. "You're doing fine, Carc," said Olaus. "Now, I want you and Mommy to sit here a bit and rest and I'll go ahead to camp and get a fire started. Right up this little slope and down the other side is camp, so take your time. And don't worry about Chimo; we'll find him tomorrow."

We were glad enough to dump our loads for a while, glad to know that the end was within reach. It was almost dark, and very quiet here in the high hills. The only sound was the subdued music of a little stream far below. Suddenly Donald grabbed my arm: "Mommy, listen!"

A sound as of someone breathing very hard; it came closer.

"Chimo, Chimo," called Donald, and a dark object came puffing and panting up through the grass of that steep slope and catapulted into Donald's arms, whimpering and crying with joy and almost carrying them both back down the slope in his exultation.

Donald's first word was: "Come on, let's go find Daddy!"

The packs weighed nothing, our breathing was easy, our muscles had ceased to ache. We went up that slope and, fairly running in the almost dark, went down the other side, where we saw a gleam of a tent, both of us crying: "We found Chimo; we have Chimo!"

A happy supper by a bright fire, a glad sharing of our meal with the dog, who lay as close to Donald's side as was possible. Left us he had, but he had also found us; not bad for a six-month-old puppy in entirely strange and rugged territory. As for the problem of how to feed him, he solved that in his own way—not only for himself but for us too.

Olaus was eager to get into the mountain-sheep country, and early next morning we were on our way up the long draw which led from the camp meadow upward to the great mesa-plateau extending our behind the rocky Indian profile and the top of Sheep Mountain. We skirted big snowdrifts still unmelted from the winter snowpack, jumped over streams, crossed meadows, always upward. And we began to see many wood-chucks; this was their country and at this season the young were about two-thirds grown. Suddenly Chimo left Donald's heels and went streaking across a grassy slope gaining and gaining on a young woodchuck. In two seconds he had him by the throat

and had dispatched him. Olaus called, very calmly: "Here, Chimo."

And the dog came, proudly bearing his trophy, and laid it at Olaus's feet. "Well," laughed Olaus, "I guess your dog has solved his food problem, Carc. And did you know young woodchuck is real good eating, for us too?"

"It is?" skeptically, from me.

"Why sure, why not? They eat nothing but this good vegetation."

Of course he was right. That evening we had fricasseed leg of woodchuck, and Chimo had the rest. It tasted like fried chicken. Chimo went on having a marvelous time, and the strain was removed from our laboriously transported food stores. No more shots were fired.

We had twelve beautiful days. Jackson Hole was giving us that year a perfect July, as usual—cool mornings, bright sunshine, warm noons, beauty and harmony on every side.

There is a rhythm in life out in the hills, like the movements of a symphony, like the rhythm of life. The mornings start at a slow pace, with effort. First the effort of crawling out of the sleeping bag and starting anything. Donald was a beginning Boy Scout; he had entered into an agreement with his father, which I am sure he later regretted, that he would start the fire every morning during this trip. Some mornings I lay in mental misery, but saying nothing, as I listened to Olaus's gentle but persistent prodding of that sleepy nine-year-old. Eventually, out of the bag he crawled, and out of the tent, and I would hear the crackle of a fire and know it was safe for me to get up and start breakfast. By this time the boy and the dog would be playing and rolling about together, ready for the day, ready for breakfast.

The tempo began to increase a little then, as we cleaned up the breakfast things and packed our lunch, made camp snug against any sudden storm, and started up toward the top. Every morning, an hour or more of climbing up through the long draw above our little meadow to the tops where the sheep lived. Each morning the tempo slowed as we plodded upward; each morning I thought my muscles should be tougher than the day before, but they still protested. After all, we were climbing at an altitude just under 11,000 feet; I kept consoling myself with this thought.

In this setting belongs the white-crowned sparrow with his simple little song, the song that always meant so much to Olaus and me, for it is the voice of interior Alaska in summer. And if you can get near, he is no mean personage either, with his erect military posture, his striking black and white striped crown, and vigorous movements. Here too we found the robin, but I didn't think of lawns and angleworms. Olaus and I have found this friend far out in the wilderness so many times that we no longer marveled at seeing him at the last trees; indeed we had come to associate him with timberline, and at our camp, in the grove of trees by the little stream, he was the first singer of the dawn.

But every day we reached the lovely moderato of the mesa, and the hours up there were pure joy. This part of the world of Jackson Hole is a miles-long and miles-wide plateau, or mesa, extending out to the heads of Flat Creek, Granite Creek, Cache Creek, and the Gros Ventre River—they all come to a meeting up there behind the Sleeping Indian. The mesa is a succession of alpine meadows dotted with the blue and white and gold and purple of every kind of alpine flower, and cut into at all sorts of angles by canyons. We would be hiking along over the bright flower-garden turf, a pleasure to walk on, and come to a sudden stop at the brink of a cliff, the perpendicular walls of some side canyon.

There is plenty of room up here. Veering away from the heads of these canyons, we still had miles of sheep country to explore. Olaus would gain some little ridge and sit with his binoculars scanning all around him, and the boy and the dog and I would sit quietly waiting nearby. Pretty soon: "Well, there's a band. Hmm-m, about twenty-eight I think—ewes and lambs. We'll just wait."

We lay on the soft turf and waited, hats over faces, for the sun was hot though there were always cool gentle breezes up here. After a while Olaus, who had been alternately writing notes or sketching, and watching, would announce: "All right; they have moved on. We can go over now and see what they were eating."

We would all hike to the spot, drop to our knees, and start crawling about, looking for any plant that had been nipped off, each of us taking a different small area to work in but close enough to call out to Olaus what we found so he could list it in his notebook. We had had from him a short intensive course on the more common plants of the area. We often laughed at the thought of what some stranger would think, suddenly coming upon this scene: three people and a dog sniffing about on hands and knees and calling out: "Bistort, dryas, anemone, another bistort."

Donald soon found a new method of tracking down what the sheep had been eating. He watched Chimo and noticed that every time the dog's nose went down to sniff, there was a stem of something nipped off. To a dog's senses, mountain sheep must leave plenty of aroma behind. This was a game we enjoyed. We also enjoyed helping make the counts of every band of sheep, and locating the bands too. Donald and I were both keen to see if we could spot a band off in the distance on a green slope before Olaus did. We were not often able to do it; but once in a while we did. Even so, I still wonder if perhaps he had not seen them first with his practiced eye and just waited, to let us have the thrill. It would be like him, but I never asked. For me, it was a joy to hear Donald's voice suddenly: "I see some sheep."

Then we would find a good place to sit down, and each in turn be given the glasses, and make his count, and finally compare notes and enter the number in the notebook: 27, 32, 14. I don't recall that we ever saw more than 32 in a band up there. Something mysterious was happening to the mountain sheep of Jackson Hole in those years. In 1929 the Forest Service had made a census of about 1,200. Then after that they seemed to be decreasing. Olaus had been given this assignment since the elk study was drawing to a close; the report, a thick book entitled *The Elk of North America*, was almost finished. With scientists and field men from the the State of Wyoming and the Forest Service, the sheep study went on for several years more, and the conclusion was that the cause of the decline was, not the coyote, but pneumonia in the young lambs, due to lungworm. Perhaps this is all a part of a natural cycle with these animals, for the mountain sheep have been slowly building up again in numbers. And if the high rugged wilderness ranges can only be kept as they are, I feel sure these beautiful animals of the timberline will always be there where they belong, to give a special pleasure to all who care to make the effort to get to know this precious part of Jackson Hole.

How delicious every crumb of food tastes on a mountain! Our food was the simplest, but many a time in years afterward Olaus and I recalled the fun of lunches high up on the mesa in the sheep summer ranges. We had knäckebröd, and cheddar cheese, and raisins and dried peaches or apricots, and a few Fig Newtons or sometimes a candy bar. There was no water up there on top, but nearly always in some sheltered nook we would find a snowdrift and dig into its clean interior and make a snow- or iceball and sit happily sucking it. No mineral value, no iodine, but at least moisture for a dry throat.

The tempo of the day would be slowing as we trudged home, but it was a peaceful slow tempo, without effort, going downhill. And part way down, Donald and Chimo would give us a presto movement for a few moments. At one side of the draw about halfway down was a large snowdrift, perhaps an acre in extent, sloping down from the wall of the little valley at an angle which made sliding just fast enough to be exciting, and the boy and the dog knew exactly what to do. They got on the drift at its top, and went into a great tussle, just as they had done on the linoleum floor at home from the time Chimo was a tiny puppy. The rules were well understood. Chimo was to growl, and to chew at Donald's overalls, or his flannel shirt-sleeve, and try to drag him. But he was never to bite through the cloth or take hold of bare flesh, and he never did. At home this great mock battle took place on the floor. Here it was on a sloping snowdrift, and the contestants as they growled and chuckled were sliding toward the bottom, going round and round, rolling over and over, finally ending in a big schuss into the green turf at the bottom.

After fifteen minutes or so of this fun, they were ready to trot on down over the grassy slopes to camp, drying off in the late afternoon sun, and perhaps catching another woodchuck on the way. Thus the symphony of the day slowed to an adagio as they both lay contentedly side by side near the evening fire and watched me cook supper. Later, when we were snug in our sleeping bags, with Chimo at our feet, Olaus would read a chapter from *The Jungle Book* by the light of two candles side by side. No matter how heavy the packs, we never went into camp without books.

In many ways we were on the heights during those twelve days of July.

20

The Falcon

{{ O·M }}

The next excitement after our return from Sheep Mountain was the delivery of a seventeen-foot Oldtown canoe for which the whole family had saved their pennies. The boys and I set it up on a trestle in the back yard and I painted a black and gold falcon head on its bow. We hoped the canoe would cleave the waters as the falcon did the air. For the rest of that summer all our free days were spent on the various lakes of Jackson Hole; the boys even taught Chimo to sit quietly in the canoe, though he always laid his prick ears down and looked quite unhappy. Chimo liked to swim but didn't take to boating.

For the next summer the boys and I planned something different. Martin was about to go away to college; there was also a war looming black. We had a hunger for a real adventure by canoe before Martin left home. Donald, only ten, seemed to be a direct descendant of Mardy's seagoing ancestors and was eager about anything connected with boats and water.

On a sunny calm morning in July we loaded our duffle into the car, lashed The Falcon on top, and headed north.

I had seen the Upper Yellowstone in places, like a line here and there in a poem, pages apart; enough to guess its character. When you go into country by pack train the streams are only for crossing, or to camp beside. To know a stream you travel on it, struggle with it, live with it hour by hour and day by day.

That first day we accepted a lift by Park Service motorboat across the great sweep of Yellowstone Lake. That part could not count, and I even had a vague uneasy sense of guilt that we had not crossed by the efforts of our own paddles. Our jumping-off place, then, was near the end of the Southeast Arm, where we lowered the canoe into the water, loaded in our duffle, waved goodbye to the rangers, and paddled off for a look at the Molly Islands.

These are two low insignificant specks that would hardly be worthy of a place on the map were it not for their feathered inhabitants. The first one was swarming with screaming gulls which rose in the air like a swirling white cloud as though a large feather bed had burst upon the wind. Among the milling California gulls we noted the black heads and red beaks of a few Caspian terns, and on the low ridge of the island the black silhouette of a nest of cormorants.

When we left this noisy confetti-like spot and paddled to the other island we found an entirely different atmosphere. Here was quiet, and a company of voiceless dignified white pelicans. As we came near, a group of them waddled off uneasily and finally took wing, leaving a huddle of woolly lamb-like young birds. These solemnly marched in a long line from one end of the island to the other, and there bunched together again in stupid uncertainty. Some of them reacted to danger in characteristic fashion—they deliberately and clumsily spewed up their dinner. A few alert gulls had anticipated this and swooped down upon the discarded food.

The two boys gazed wonderingly at this spectacle. They had never before seen the white pelicans in numbers like this, or the California gull in such dense population. The cameras came into play and we lingered a bit, slowly drifting along close to the shore; but this was not why we had come and we did not want to disturb the pelican colony too long. We looked to the forested shoreline, to the gap in the mountains whence we knew came the river, and Beaverdam Creek, and Trail Creek. Somewhere over there toward shore, geese were calling, and we caught the flash of wings. Life and adventure lay yonder: the rim of a new world for us.

We found a break in the shoreline, a small stream coming out from a shallow inlet, and nosed The Falcon up into an almost hidden pond. It was as though we had touched an unseen spring or spoken the magic word and had suddenly found ourselves in a world of fairy folk. A group of gulls were here too, however, wading at the far end. What were they doing here? We paddled along the shore of this quiet, shaded waterway. Where the gulls had been feeding we found nothing but tadpoles. Was that their fare?

Farther on we startled a newly hatched brood of mallards, and a few moments later some downy young geese scuttled into the long grass ahead of the canoe, and as we turned and headed out of this secluded spot a little raft of dark heads swirled ahead of us, a family of buffleheads.

Coming out into the main lake, we had to face a little rough water crossing to the mouth of the Yellowstone, but The Falcon took it easily. Martin and I were paddling; Donald trolled a spinner and caught six nice trout, including one 14½ inches long. This was enough to enable him to ignore the mosquitoes which swarmed about us until we had our cooking fire built. We camped in a clump of spruce above a sandy beach on the fourth or fifth bend of the river above its mouth. It is a winding stream here, and pretty swift, but the paddling was not hard. I am sure the boys were wondering whether we would have mosquitoes with us all the way upriver, but as it turned out our other camps were on bars or open shores where we could almost forget the bugs. Here in our first camp we sat near the smoke and filled ourselves with delicious trout and pooled our memories of the birds we had seen this day, including ospreys. I noted something I had not been aware of before: the six nests we had already counted in that short stretch of river were in three pairs; in each case there was a nest on either side of the river.

In the morning we quickly gained the river valley proper and the clear water of the Upper Yellowstone. This part of the river is a mountain stream, relatively small, fast, with steep slopes bordering it closely, quite different from the part that begins at Fishing Bridge and flows through the broad shallow Hayden Valley on its way to the Grand Canyon. The boys this day learned about sweepers—trees or logs extending from the shore into the current. In a small stream there is little room to maneuver and the danger of being swept against a sweeper, and under, is especially great. To me it brought back memories of streams in Labrador and Alaska, and my sons got quite a long lecture on caution and alertness as we all bent to the paddles. Some of the sweepers were trees still vigorous and alive, spruces for example, which held the banks with their roots and whose trunks and green boughs were continually thrummed by the current. It was frightening to have to work close to a tree which was being played this way by the river.

There was only one short rapid this day, a bit of white water at a right-angle bend. This stretch had to be lined, and thereafter we found ourselves lining much of the time; we were truly going up the stream. I suppose I felt, after all my years in Canada and Alaska, that no one could line a canoe as well as I, or perhaps I felt it was good experience for the boys to handle the canoe. Most of the time this is the way we did it; they kept the canoe headed right and guided it around obstacles while I walked the shore with the line. Yet sometimes we found we could paddle along the edges of fast water, taking advantage of eddies at the bends or behind driftwood barriers. The boys were soon "figuring" the current, and the best routes, and I was proud of them.

Traveling slowly as we were, close to the water, we were also close to all the little hidden places along the banks and under the water; trout in deep holes lined with colored stones, a mink track in damp sand, water striders on small coves formed

by miniature sand or gravel spits, and over our heads, in the thick alder brush and willows, there seemed to be always a yellow warbler. Each bend opened a scene to explore, and long afterward, when the boys and I were reminiscing, we agreed that we nearly always had a little flock of young buffleheads or American mergansers ahead of the canoe.

The five days up the river were days of hard work, but lightened by our feeling of exploration, of curiosity, and the diversions of the birds, the animals, the fish. We had soon figured our method of travel and had settled down to the fun of exploring. Each evening before dark, at a carefully selected camp spot, we would find our position on the map and as we ticked off the landmarks passed—Trapper's Creek, Mountain Creek, Cliff Creek—we would speculate on the unknown ahead. The boys caught trout for our supper, and a couple of times they dove into the river for a short swim. It was always a short one, and they never even asked me to come on in; they knew how I hate cold water.

Above Cliff Creek the water was easier but the river began to wind a lot. Our fifth day was a gloomy one; we got out into the grassland and the river split up into channels and we came to a logjam that we had to carry around. It began to seem interminable, no woods around, the afternoon waning, no good campground in sight, and this was mosquito country. But gradually the stream drew over toward the west side of the big valley, toward the mountains. We passed the mouth of Thorofare at last, and came into a section of the river beautiful beyond words. The mosquitoes were out in swarms, there were baffling shallows, but we could not help enjoying the grassy banks, the trees, and the pleasant windings of the stream. Then we came to a thin strip of woods that promised some breeze and we decided: "This is camp. This is our kind of country."

We had worked our way safely out of the hostile slough country. And when the evening cold laid the mosquitoes low, we were sitting happily by our fire, watching two bull moose in the willows below camp. Then Donald brought out the maps to the campfire light, and we realized that we had reached the mouth of Falcon Creek and what appeared to be the head of canoe navigation. How appropriate that The Falcon should have reached Falcon Creek! We knew that Bridger Lake was only a short hike from here.

In the morning we set out afoot for the lake. It was strange and in a way a relief to leave the river for a while. After we crossed a wide complex of meadow and willow, and found a trail through the pines, the sound of running water disappeared; the world seemed altogether quiet.

At the lake began hours of photographic adventure. We were able to get both movies and stills of cow moose with calf, bull moose, moose swimming, all at close range. Donald was given the big Graflex to operate, while I used the movie camera. Martin was busy with his precious Rolleiflex, which we had given him for graduation. All this was not as simple as mere words imply. Try to stalk a cow and calf moose feeding in a lake. When the heads of both animals were underwater, we could move toward them; when one head cleared the surface for a breath, we had to freeze in position. The skill in this game is in predicting the moose's movements so that you do not have to freeze in an impossibly awkward position. Try to avoid being trapped into immobility while on one foot in unstable mud, looking at the world through the ground glass screen of a heavy camera.

We finally returned to camp through a long meadow ablaze with wild flowers, triumphant over a lot of exposed film, and delighted that we had been able to leave the lake while mother and calf were still feeding peacefully, all unaware.

Back at camp I made bannock with the pancake flour and

we had canned beef and vegetables, and prunes, and honey on the bannock, and a lot of good talk by the fire—movies we had seen, actors we enjoyed, adventurers we most admired, our own adventures. Tomorrow we would start the swift descent of the river. So far as we knew, no one else had ever come this far up the Yellowstone by canoe.

The morning was clear and cool. We made a snug load, most of it covered with a tarp, and The Falcon slipped along the shadowy banks in perfect harmony with the river. Suddenly a beaver was there with us, floating downstream between our right gunwale and the grassy overhang of a bank. He apparently accepted us as part of the normal traffic of the river; he was less than a paddle length away, his whiskers, his wetted fur and dark eyes vividly clear. This was altogether different from the usual view of beaver from a higher vantage point on shore or bank.

We saw other animals in the same way—mergansers, goldeneyes, buffleheads, and warblers too, but the beaver stands out in memory. And the grizzly too. Meeting him was an adventure that still seems too bizarre to be true.

We had safely passed over half of the downstream distance, we thought, and had become accustomed to the navigation hazards and the slight worry over new challenges that could sweep into view at each bend. I know the boys felt their initiation period was over; we had even run the little rapids at the right-angle bend, and many a sweeper lay behind, successfully avoided. As a new stretch of river opened before us, we made the routine quick check of the banks—all was comparatively clear—and we did not see the bear swimming in mid-stream until we were coming down on him, too close to change course. I don't remember what we said to one another, or if we could think to say anything; I only remember trying to back-paddle for lack of any other possible action. It was clear that we were going to overtake the bear; the current was too fast for us to cross quickly enough to one side.

The grizzly solved the situation. We saw his head turn slightly. He had become aware of us and he managed an increase in speed that seemed incredible, arrived at shallow water where he could get footing just as we swept by, and galloped up the bank, shedding great sheets of water as he went. As Donald said, he "seemed to take half the river with him." And we gave him a great shout of relief to speed him on his way as we slid on down the stream.

Late in the afternoon we knew we were approaching the delta; the fast water was behind us; we could remember no bad stretches from this point on down. Suddenly the river made a very sharp turn to the left and there we saw a long tangle of sweepers and driftwood. We had of course passed this place on the far side going up, none of us even remembered it, but I knew at once that we were in trouble. "Paddle for all you're worth!" I shouted, and put all the power I could in my stern paddle, but we were allowed only a few seconds.

Then the boiling undercurrent at the edge of the drift pile flipped the canoe over and we were underwater. I shall never forget the strange rushing sound of that water as we went over. As I swam upward my head bumped on the bottom of the canoe, and I had to swim out to the side to get up. It seemed like the slow movements of a nightmare and I was terrified about the boys. But I needn't have been. When I finally came spluttering and gasping to the surface and flung an arm over the canoe, there was Martin clinging to the bow and grinning at me, and there just opposite me was Donald, still with his precious white "gob hat" on his head, and holding something aloft with one hand: "I've got Martin's camera!"

A moment later I don't think he could have shouted that or anything. We were all so stunned with the shock of the cold water we could not speak, but we were all there, and The Falcon was with us still and we had been carried clear of the dreadful drift pile. Without words we knew what we had to do. We clung to the canoe and swam as hard as we could till we touched bottom and managed to pull up on the beach, and as we went Martin reached out and grabbed a paddle that was floating by. Later we found another one, stuck in the middle of the drift pile, and Martin crawled out and retrieved it.

Two packsacks were still in the canoe, tied to the thwarts, and Donald had Martin's camera; he had felt something bump his knees as we went over, and had reached and grabbed a strap, but my tried and true Graflex with the seventeen-inch lens, veteran of thousands of miles of travel in the north, was gone to the bottom, and the kit of camp utensils, along with some other things of lesser value, including two good trout caught at our lunch stop that noon. We swiftly unpacked and spread things to dry. The first thing to check was the exposed film, and this seemed to be dry. But the matches were soaked. Donald set them upright in a crack of a log to dry, but the sun was already low; how my waterproof match safe had got out of my pocket none of us ever knew.

We were shivering violently as we frantically unrolled duffle. Suddenly I remembered the map inside my notebook in its rubber case inside my shirt. We spread it out and saw that there was a Park Service ranger cabin a short distance downstream. I felt in my pocket and gleefully discovered I still had my key ring, and that key ring through all the years of my studies of the elk had had on it a master key to the Park Service cabins. We dumped everything back into the canoe any old way and were glad of the exercise of a swift paddle downstream. By dusk we had found the cabin, nestled unobtrusively in spruce timber a quarter of a mile from the river.

What a fine evening that was, once we had a roaring fire in the little stove and had pretty well dried ourselves out. We had no tools, but the cabin did, and we cooked the last of our food, some oatmeal. It was soaked, but that didn't matter; we cooked it and Donald found a can of syrup open on one of the shelves in the cabin. We didn't want to open up their emergency rations, but we thought it would be all right to use a bit of syrup on our oatmeal.

On the wall was a telephone, presumably connected with Lake Ranger Station. Somehow we hated to crank that phone and have the adventure end.

When the Ranger launch contacted us the next day in the delta area, and the canoe was loaded on board, we lashed it down carefully with a feeling of affection. After all, though a structure of wood and canvas, The Falcon had been the means of our adventure and had performed beautifully.

The next evening we were at home. Chimo rushed to greet us when we drove in at dusk, but no one else was there. We got the stuff unloaded. We piled some of the soaked gear in a heap in the front vestibule. A few moments later I heard the front door open, and Mardy's voice: "Oh my goodness, you're home—wonderful! But what on earth is all this?"

And then I heard Donald's slow quiet voice as I started down the stairs: "Don't start squawkin' until you've heard the whole story!"

There was a moment of silence. Then: "O.K.—suppose I make a pot of hot cocoa."

It was pretty wonderful, a little bit later, to sit there in the cozy dining room in clean dry clothes, and to tell her and Joanne "the whole story."

21

Dude Ranch Summers

M · M

In a way, the canoe trip marked the end of a chapter. Those were the last isolated years, years when the valley was a world to itself, when our children, all the children, were growing up in a special atmosphere of freedom, nurtured by the affection and relaxed tolerance of the whole community.

But Pearl Harbor had found us too. December 1943 saw us trying to follow our serene pattern of life but at the same time feeling the bludgeoning of war, as were all American homes. The Gang of the Mountains were all gone to the Army, at eighteen. Our dear friend Severine had gone to Laramie and established a home where her older boys had been going to college and where now they could come from the ski-troops training camp, Camp Hale, Colorado, and our Martin with them, whenever they could get a pass. It was natural that Martin and Harold and his brother Grant, and eight or ten other Jackson

Hole boys, should volunteer for the Tenth Mountain Infantry—they had grown up on skis and climbing the hills at an altitude of 6,300 feet and more.

Joanne had gone to Seattle to my older brother and his family for her third year of high school. Olaus and Donald and Chimo and I were at home; the last revision of *The Elk of North America* was nearly finished.

My friends and I kept ourselves busy knitting and sewing for the Red Cross and baking and packing food to be sent to camp to the boys, and working in our own hospital, where Olaus was also spending his overtime hours, for he had been persuaded to act as Superintendent of the hospital in the wartime emergency. The fine doctor who had come to the valley after Dr. Huff's death said to us: "You girls can do a lot of things you didn't think you could do."

He and his colleague soon showed us the truth of this. I said I would wash dishes and peel vegetables, but pretty soon I was bathing patients or scrubbing the operating room.

Each night, by the fireplace, Olaus and Donald and I, with Chimo at our feet, listened to the news on the radio. We knew that Martin and Harold and Grant and all the others would soon be going overseas. We were like a little band of wapiti in a blizzard, huddled close to one another for warmth and comfort and dreading what the outside world would send us next. There was no escape for anyone in those days; the only saving thing was to keep very busy.

So in this great need to be busy, to save myself from the thoughts that swirled in my head all the time, I sat down with

Olaus one day in early spring to reread a letter which had come from our dear friend Margaret Huyler in Connecticut. Would I consider taking on the job of housekeeper for the Bear Paw, their dude ranch in Jackson Hole? I would have a room and bath in the building which also held the office and linen room; they would expect Olaus to use the ranch as his headquarters also; Joanne could have a job as waitress if she wished, and they would want her to ride and hike right along with the other young guests; and Donald could be the assistant chore boy if he wanted to work.

"Well," said Olaus, "I think maybe it would be a good thing; you need to be busy; I'm going to be in Yellowstone off and on quite a bit on that bear study [as Olaus put it, he was trying to find out how to make the bears safe from the tourists], and think how wonderful it will be for Joanne to be with horses again, she's always been so crazy about them."

This decision changed the course of our lives, though we did not guess it at the time. I plunged gratefully into carrying out all the suggestions which came from Margaret and Coulter. I enticed our good friend Howard away from the Forest Service to be the new foreman; I found a lively schoolteacher with a wonderful sense of humor who was also a fine cook. She had never cooked for forty-two people, but was willing to try. Severine's sister Klara, another teacher, agreed to come and work as chief cabin girl; Joanne wrote from Seattle in enthusiastic agreement. In late May, Howard and I began moving up to the ranch and our house in town was rented to friends from Illinois for the summer.

The Bear Paw was one of the finest dude ranches in the valley. It had first been the summer home of the Huylers— Easterners who had become true Westerners—and had later been turned into an operating dude ranch. Its situation was superb, actually on the lower slopes of the Tetons, on the west side of the valley. The buildings, all log, were on a slight rise looking out over the whole valley to Sheep Mountain directly across and seeming to loom high in the sky. Our two summers there were memorable; I never worked so hard in my life, or had more fun, or learned more about people.

The Huylers maintained the highest standards of fine, simple, Western life for their guests. They were keenly interested in young people, and about half the guests were youngsters from fourteen to eighteen. Most of them came from wealthy families of course, but all were treated with firmness, with kindness. Joanne found herself working in the dining room with the daughter of one of the most prominent men in New York, who felt it was more fun to work, washing dishes, setting tables, waiting on tables, while still paying dude rates, than to be just a guest. She and Joanne and the third waitress did their work at top speed in order to be ready to ride with the rest of the young folks every morning and every afternoon.

I can see them now, three beautiful young things, hair flying in the breeze, racing down the grassy slope through the scarlet gilia blossoms to be on time at the corral; to ride down the valley or up the valley, or up into one of the canyons of the Tetons. They would be back in time to clean up and come tearing into the dining room to set the table for lunch; they would

rush to clear the tables and wash the dishes; they might possibly go to their big cabin, where eight girls roomed, and be
relatively quiet for a few minutes, but then it would be time for
the afternoon ride.

As I rushed from one task to another, I would hear the
young chatter and laughter fading away in the aspen grove, and
an old nursery song always came into my head: "Boys and
girls together; in the sunny weather."

When the afternoon ride came back, they must swim, in
the natural swimming pool behind the main house; then there
was dinner to set and serve and wash up from, and if it were not
too dark, a game of ping-pong out on the terrace behind the

dining room, or volleyball in the meadow below. Finally, into the huge living room, to play games at one end of the room, or to gather at the piano at the other end with Margaret and sing songs with her, or to curl up on the big buffalo rugs before the fireplace and listen to Howard singing songs with his banjo, until 9:30 curfew hour arrived and they were all banished to their cabins so the grown-ups could have a half hour of quiet talk before lights out. And on Friday night Howard and Harry the wrangler, and the boy guests, cleared the dining room after dinner and we all danced.

To the youngsters it was all one long glad song, punctuated and spiced by young love. (If the girls were not in love with some of the boy guests, they could easily fall in love with the cowboys!) To Coulter and Margaret, to Margaret's sweet Scottish secretary Mary, to Howard and to me, there were also all the details of keeping things just so for the guests and never letting them know there was ever any stress or strain. Margaret and Coulter had to deal with the idiosyncrasies of guests; Howard and I had this too, but he also had horses to think of, and the light plant, and the plumbing.

I had to see that the cabins were kept immaculate, that supplies were always on hand, that laundry was collected and sorted and listed and sent, and picked up in town and sorted again and put away; that the cook was kept happy, that the food was excellent, that the menus had variety—and all this on wartime rationing.

No day went as I thought it would. My alarm went off at 6:30. At seven I was in the living room, cleaning it for the day's use, carpet sweeper over the seven Navajo rugs and the two buffalo hides, dust mop all round the edges, dust the furniture. As I ran the dustcloth over the piano keys, Howard's voice from the other side of the wall, in the kitchen: "Play it again! Then come on in and have a cup of coffee."

Howard, big, blond, confident, blue eyes sparkling, would be at the long table at the end of the kitchen. "Even my dog goes around with his tail between his legs till I've had my first cup of coffee!"

But this was our last moment of quiet all day long, and even while we drank the coffee I would be checking the day's menu once more with Marylee, and Howard and his good right hand Harry would be deciding which horses had to be shod that morning before the ride. Time now to join Margaret and Mary and the guests out under the big pine tree by the front door for morning prayers.

Perhaps I thought to get the big picture window in the end of the dining room cleaned right after breakfast, but there was Klara: "What shall we do with Mrs. Rideout? She wants a different kind of lamp on her writing table and I can't find any extras in the storeroom."

Before that extra lamp is found, another worried dude stops me in the path: "You know, I'm sure I felt a mouse run right over my bed last night. I hardly slept a wink after that!"

I reassured the guest. Charlie or Donald would set traps in her cabin—I started for the linen room; it was laundry day. As I went through the office, Nola, Harry's wife, who was our sweet gentle-voiced bookkeeper, looked up from her ledger:

"Mrs. Van called to say she just can't spare ten chickens for this Sunday. And Lucie wants you to call her—she needs to be paid right away for the cream and eggs."

Now the laundry— No, not yet. Joanne, booted and hatted, ready for riding, and out of breath: "Mommy, Marylee says tell you those cantaloupe are all spoiled. You'll have to find something else for dessert this noon. Sorry, I have to run."

Rush back to the kitchen, to the big pantry behind it. "Marylee, can you find time to make a simple custard, and we'll put these canned peaches on it?"

At last, to the linen room; one of the boys would be leaving soon with the small truck for town. Where was the grocery list for him?

Lunchtime—help dish up the custards. It would feel wonderful to get back to my room and lie down for just half an hour. But before the half hour is up, I hear the truck pull up outside. The finished laundry from last trip to town is being delivered and I must help Klara put it away. At the door stood Coulter, his gray moustache fairly bristling with good humor and charm. He had been in town, too, that morning. "Mardy, you know I met a wonderful charming fellow in town, an Army colonel; he's been on some special perilous mission—"

Coulter paused. I knew what was coming. "But Coulter, there isn't a single vacant *crack* on this ranch right now!"

"Yes, I know, Mardy, but he only has four days, and seeing who he is, and all our boys overseas—seemed to me it was our patriotic duty . . ." He paused. "You know, there's Mary's little cabin—and he doesn't want to be in town; he wants to be on a ranch."

Two hours later, sweet long-suffering Mary had vacated her cabin. We had carried her things to Marylee's cabin, where the only vacant bed on the place was, and Klara had cheerfully given her hours off to making the cabin ready for the colonel. (I suppose it was worth it. The colonel came and was delighted, and he was personable and lively and sophisticated, and gave all the girls some excitement for four days.)

A fairly typical day at the Bear Paw. But before it ended, I would probably have to go find Donald at the swimming hole and remind him it was time to build all the coal fires at all the cabins, for the guests' baths; and then try to help Nola balance the checkbook. She knew more about it than I did, but liked moral support. And there would be a guest who "couldn't understand a thing that agent at Rock Springs was saying on the phone, and would you call back, Mardy? Tell him I just must have a bedroom all the way to New York!"

Whenever Olaus came down from Yellowstone for a few days he was kept busy too. All the guests, young and old, soon fell under his quiet spell. At Coulter's urging, he told them stories; he answered their questions; he took them on walks in the summer dusk; he imitated bird and animal calls for them. If he tried to hide away in my room to work on an official report, there would be the voice of a guest in the office asking Nola: "Where is Dr. Murie? He promised to show me that plant we were talking about last night."

These were wealthy people who all their lives had been able to command whatever material thing they thought they wanted. And they had ridden the trails and looked at the scenery from atop a horse. But here was someone showing them a simpler kind of joy: tracks of mice, of toads, or badger or elk, in the dust of the trail; the winter burrows of pocket gophers, the hay piles of conies in the rock slides; the stories to be read in the aspens, where bears had ripped the bark to eat the cambium layer and lick the sap, and where moose had scraped upward with their teeth for the same purpose.

One evening Olaus took a group, both old and young, for a walk up the creek which tumbled out of Granite Canyon behind the ranch, and as they turned back he said: "You know, you can pretty well feel your way with your feet if you ever get caught out after dark. Let's all close our eyes and see if we can go all the way back to the ranch." And they did.

In our second summer at the Bear Paw, Margaret had in her charge eleven-year-old daughters of two very well-known families. They were younger, and they were put to bed earlier than the others, and one evening Joanne and her friends came to Olaus: "Daddy, come on over to the little girls' cabin, will you, and hide in the trees outside, and howl like a coyote and hoot like an owl? They haven't heard a coyote yet, and we promised them they'd howl tonight."

I wonder if these little girls, now long grown up and I know not where, by chance remember a soft summer night on the Bear Paw, and a coyote howling and a great horned owl talking outside in the darkness?

What *I* remember most poignantly from those summers are the days of departure, a time Margaret dreaded. After my first September there, I knew why she did.

At breakfast three or four guests would come in dressed

in city clothes, and with sad faces. After breakfast the car would be taking them to the railroad. If they were young folks, faces were even sadder, and streaked with tears. They looked uncomfortable in their city clothes, while those who had another week or more to stay, still in bright shirts and Levi's, looked a bit smug, but the shadow was creeping up on them too. No one ever wanted to leave. Here these wealthy people's children had a free and simple and richly active life that was probably not possible at home.

They did not want to say goodbye to the valley, the ranch, the crew, their companions—most of all, their horses. On the morning the Stinnetts were to leave, Harry had to bring the ten-year-old daughter's pony up to the cabin to say goodbye, and when all the bags were in the car and the driver waiting, the little girl still stood, face buried in the pony's mane, weeping. It was Olaus who gently pulled her away and put her into the car.

No one wanted to leave. I didn't either. I didn't want to go back to town.

22

A New Life

M·M

In the middle of the second summer at Bear Paw, the Gang of the Mountains came home. Martin and Harold had both been wounded in Italy, but they were home again now, trying to adjust to the life-and-business-as-usual attitude of the country they thought they had been saving.

And about this same time Olaus had a long-distance call from Washington, D.C.

For ten years he had been a member of the Council of The Wilderness Society, founded in 1935 by Bob Marshall and his friends who felt, with him, that "there is just one hope of repulsing the tyrannical ambition of civilization to conquer every niche on the whole earth. That hope is the organization of spirited people who will fight for the freedom of wilderness."

After Bob's sudden and untimely death, Olaus had been amazed to learn that he had been named a trustee of the will also. Now Robert Sterling Yard, the president, was gone too, and the Executive Committee, through our old friend Robert Griggs, David's father, was calling.

Olaus and I sat down in my room at the Bear Paw and looked at each other. "I told Robert I just could not take the job of Director; I can't live in a city, so I guess that's that. You agree, don't you?"

"Yes, I know you can't live in a city. But it would be the happiest day of my life if you left government service. The big elk study is done—what project can they offer you now that will really be a challenge to your talents? I know there must be plenty of studies, but the government doesn't seem to be financing or planning any right now. I feel you're just marking time. Most anybody could tell the Park Service what they ought to do about those bears!"

Next day another call from Washington. Robert said: "We may be able to get Howard Zahniser to take over the work here as Executive Secretary, and you know how good he is. How about your taking the job as Director, but at half time and half pay, and stay in Wyoming?"

So—a new work, a new job. But not only that. A new home too, a whole new life, a whole new career.

I did not want to go back to town. The Bear Paw had spoiled me. I wanted to live where I could walk out of the door and into the woods. All the years we had been living in the valley I had had a special feeling for a special piece of forest, beaver ponds, and river, the seventy-seven acres which were the STS dude ranch of Buster and Frances, our companions of so many adventures. Now they were thinking of moving to Arizona.

Just two months after the phone calls from Washington we, with Adolph and Louise, were the owners of the STS. Ade and Weezy had come back to the valley from a field assignment in the Southwest just in time to say: "Why don't we buy the whole ranch"—and to move promptly onto it that same fall.

Of course we had to sell the house in town to buy the ranch. It truly was a year of "all change" in our lives, but we felt every step was a good one.

I have not been inside "the pumpkin shell" since the June day we piled the last few things into the station wagon and drove fourteen miles north to the new home a mile downriver from Moose Post Office—but every time I drive past I am grateful to the present owners for the care they give it. The spruces and cottonwoods we planted have grown tall; the lawn and the rock garden are beautifully kept.

Our friends in town no doubt thought Weezy and I slightly balmy. We were both leaving modern town houses to go up the valley where in 1945 no electric power was available and all side roads, and often the main roads, were snowed in from December until late April.

The STS had eight cabins and three houses on it, plus barn, shop, saddle house, oil shed, and storehouse. Weezy and Ade were in the long low main lodge, the original homestead cabin. In later years Buster and Frances had built another log house for themselves. Beyond all these buildings and over against some woods, but facing the mountains in the west, was a large log house belonging to a friend of Buster and Frances. In our third summer on the ranch, Olaus and I were able to buy this house for ourselves. Having lived in every other house and cabin on the ranch at times during those three years, we were finally settled in our permanent abode.

But the first winters on the ranch *were* a contrast to town life, even *simple* town life. In the late fall we stocked up on every possible staple supply and filled our cellars and cupboards. Wonderful feeling, this laying-in of plenty of stores against winter—groceries, fuel oil, gasoline, wood for fireplaces and wood ranges. Later still would come the day when the snow was deep enough so we knew it was time to park the car out at Moose on the main road a mile away, before the next storm. From then on we were snowed in for the winter, and no telephone.

Once in two weeks we would ski out, drive to town (if the car would start), get some fresh stuff, visit our friends, and hurry to get back before dark, park the car, unload the supplies, and stow them on the toboggan.

Before starting across the sagebrush flat toward the woods, we went into the one lighted log house, Carmichaels', picked up our mail, and chatted a few moments with Fran the postmistress and her husband Bob, famous flycaster and fishing guide, omnivorous reader and natural storyteller. Bob had been a newspaperman and now used this natural talent to keep track of everyone and everything from Moose to Moran. Their needs, their troubles, their humorous comments on life, love, and the weather, all came to Bob on the phone or from the neighbors dropping in for mail. Through Bob, we all knew just how our valley world was spinning. He and Fran and their telephone were our lifeline—the efficient strand keeping us in touch with the outside world. Considering that the winter population in those first years consisted of the Carmichaels and two other families at Moose Post Office, and the sixty or so Park Service folks three miles up the road at Park Headquarters, and the few people wintering on the scattered ranches, it was amazing how much happened—how much news we made. And one of Bob's frequent comments was, with a sly smile: "Nothing ever happens at Moose!"

So now, with the mail sack added to our load, to pull our skis from the snowbank where they had been standing all day and start for home, Olaus or Donald skiing and pulling, I skiing behind and pushing on the end of the toboggan with one pole. The breeze might be chilly crossing the flat, but then the trail entered the woods and it was quiet and warmer. And when in deep dusk we could see the line of thick close-ranked spired spruces on our left, we knew we were nearly home and would soon hear Chimo's happy barking from the front porch.

Home—quickly stow the skis in the corner of the porch, unload the toboggan and stand it upright in the woodshed (one soon learns at Moose that anything left down flat may be completely lost under snow by morning). Then to light the fire in the kitchen range while Olaus goes out to the shed hopefully to start the light plant; a surge of relief every time the lights blaze on.

By the time I have a meal ready, the fire in the fireplace

will be burning high, the big oil heater across the room from it will be thawing out the other corners a bit; and we can sit down gratefully at a table in front of the fire where Chimo also lies content, and eat dinner while Edward R. Murrow tells us the news.

The heart of the house which is now our home is a spacious living room with two picture windows at the front, opening on-to a large recessed porch. The room is flanked on one side by kitchen, bath, and one bedroom, on the other by three more bedrooms, and in the side wall between it and the kitchen is the massive stone fireplace wall. Behind the living room, a sep-arate wing, is a room which had been a summer dining room but which became Olaus's study.

The snow, the storms, the wood sawing and hauling and

chopping, the skiing or snowshoeing a mile for mail or messages; all this we enjoyed, and gladly paid that price for the
ineffable peace and beauty of this place which soon became
deeply *home*.

The one feature we all freely admitted was a chore was
the business of the light plant. There was one at our house, one
for the Homestead where Weezy and Ade lived whenever they
weren't away in Alaska or elsewhere on other government field
work, and one at the house Buster and Frances had built for
themselves. This latter was closed in winter, so we had only
two to worry about. But in winter there was an absolutely un-
limited number of things that could go wrong with a gasoline-
engine generator—and they did—so we were all living each day
with that nagging at the back of the mind: "Will she, won't
she, run tonight?"

Donald and Weezy were the only ones in the whole clan
who had any mechanical talent—the rest of us were not even
interested; and after two years on the ranch, Donald was away
at school. I can still see him, on his last day at home one fall,
striding out toward the light-plant shed, pliers in hand, muttering in his deep baritone: "When I leave, this place is gonna fall
apart!"

It nearly did, too, and I didn't blame Olaus or Ade for feeling frustrated to be called from their own work to figure out
why the lights flickered, or why nothing at all happened, and
then to have to go out to Moose and call for that other Bob,
Bob Kranenberg, a miracle man with any kind of ailing ma-
chinery. At such times I felt pangs of guilt for having urged
this move to the country, but always when I said, "Oh dear,

maybe we shouldn't have—" I was answered with, "Oh Mardy, of *course* we should have."

When REA arrived in Jackson Hole and extended power north from town, no one welcomed it more than we. Olaus loved to work at night, writing or drawing, and he needed good light; he had no stubborn woodsman's pride about living altogether in a primitive fashion.

People still ask, "What do you do all winter?"

After Olaus became Director of The Wilderness Society and we moved to the ranch, the days were never never long enough. Besides all the mountains of mail to be handled, on wilderness or other conservation matters—and they averaged about fifteen letters a day—Olaus was working on his book *A Field Guide to Animal Tracks* and also at times doing illustrations for other people's books. The winter day went like this:

Breakfast, often sourdough pancakes, near the crackling fire of the lovely old-fashioned wood range in the kitchen. Olaus to his long table at one side of the living room (the study could not be heated in winter in those years before we installed an oil furnace). I did dishes, made beds, planned dinner, and perhaps whipped up a dessert for it, then immediately became a secretary, taking dictation, or typing at the typewriter desk, which in winter was also in the living room, at the back window. At noon to the kitchen to fix soup or a sandwich and bring a tray to Olaus at his table. Perhaps Ade would have brought in the mail. If not, Olaus would ski or snowshoe out for it and we would sit down together to read, making notes for answers. This took at least an hour usually.

Then it was time for my outdoor adventure. It is essential,

in the long Jackson Hole winters, to get outdoors at least once a day. In the winters when Weezy and Ade and their children were on the ranch, Weezy would be with me, or Gail or Jan. I remember a lovely winter night of full moon when Gail and Jan and Weezy and I all went skiing, sliding down the little hollows, gliding across the smooth crust out on the big open flat beyond our gate, while over toward the mountains the coyotes sang to the moon.

But in midafternoon we could ski on what in summer were the trails through the woods, toward the beaver ponds, toward the mountains, or down to the willow flats along the river. Many times Weezy and I stopped suddenly and stood in silence while a moose, or two or three moose, went ambling off through the trees. This whole river bottom is their home—we are here on sufferance. It was also the home of snowshoe rabbits, of common weasel and least weasel, of beaver, otter, and mink, of porcupine and of mice, of tree squirrels and ruffed grouse, all of whom left their stories on the snow, the deep crisp perfect snow.

Every afternoon's trip provided a little story of some kind for me to report when I came skiing back to the house, where Olaus would be chopping wood at the back door. "A grouse flew out of the snow right at my feet," or "A cow moose stood and looked at us out there by the pond for about ten minutes. We thought our toes would freeze before she finally moved out of the trail so we could come home."

By now the Tetons would be shining like mammoth rugged amethysts against the clear pink winter sunset. "Going to be cold tonight," Olaus says. "I'll bring in some extra wood for the fireplace."

Feeling tinglingly alive, it was fun to hurry out of ski clothes, tie on an apron, and put some steaks on to broil. But the working day did not end with washing the dinner dishes. There was more desk work, more dictation, and then reading aloud while Olaus made some of the millions of meticulous pen strokes that created the drawings for his track book. I read George Bernard Shaw; I read Shakespeare. (I even read Pascal, but Olaus couldn't keep his mind on him.) I read Western tales, and tales of travel and natural history from all over the world.

And always all the journals of all the conservation organizations must be read. We had become immersed in the conservation battle, and enthralled and stimulated by it and by the interesting people we met in connection with it, and we both knew that life was blooming, expanding, growing because of the new work Olaus had undertaken. It demanded a great deal of us both. Correspondence was never quite caught up with; there were articles Olaus must write, lectures he must prepare, trips here and there and everywhere, to lecture, to meet, to confer, to testify, to teach, to persuade, to urge, to decide, to stand firm. To all of these he brought not only ability and talent but strength, and the desire, the involvement, the dedication. In those first winters he had also the benefit of discussing the game-preservation and conservation problems with Ade, but in the later years Ade's work for the Park Service took him to Alaska.

In the midst of these busy winter days came Christmas,

and children and friends arriving. I suppose because the big log house in the snowy woods was a perfect Christmas setting, our holidays on the ranch became rather of the old Scandinavian type, which went on for a week. I remember well a holiday when we had six dinner parties in a row, ending up with one for twenty-nine happy guests—all buffet style in the living room, by the fire, by the tree.

Christmas Eve was the special time, and here I quote from Olaus's journal of a much later year:

December 24. "This was one of those memorable days. Mardy and I woke and looked out of the window, to what a sight! All the bushes, all the aspen limbs and twigs were a white world of frost, even the big spruces were white. A soft sifting fog was dropping a thin veil of snow; but the sky was light and we knew the sun would be out soon.

"By the time we had finished our sourdough pancakes the sun was shining into this white landscape. Here we were, going into another Christmas. Mildred and Elise have both come from the East to share these days with us, Elise's first winter visit, and Adolph and Weezy are back from Alaska for the winter and are over in the homestead cabin. Soon we were all outdoors, gazing on this perfect Christmas scene, and we had our cameras, for there is always this urge to 'do something.'

"We somehow got everybody onto snowshoes. I photographed frosty bushes with dark shadows on the snow, a frosty group of aspens against the blue sky, a tall cow-parsnip plant all gleaming with frost crystals.

"Then we must go inside long enough to attend to Christmas Eve preparations, but after lunch I went out again toward the beaver ponds, came on a moose cow and calf and followed them a long time, back and forth as they wallowed through the deep snow.

"Later in the afternoon the setting sun cast a luminous golden brown on our log house, and Mildred and I took some pictures of that. Then came the deep rose and lavender of sunset, and the afterglow on the Tetons. Then I must go in and light the big fire in the fireplace, for Mickey and Bob and Reg and Gladys would soon be arriving.

"One cannot describe a Christmas Eve about a fireplace. There is so much feeling in it. There were ten of us, happy to be together. Beside the fireplace is the lighted tree—as usual, handmade by me from limbs from various large trees here in the woods. Ade and I never cut a living tree. I had carried the basis for this year's tree down from Taggart Lake, one that the trail crew had cut and thrown aside.

"Across the room we sat down at a long table decorated with a row of candles and greens, and all over the room, on the mantel among the boughs, on every bookcase, on the sideboard and in all the windows, were candles—the only electric lights were those on the tree.

"Always, Christmas Eve Norwegian supper by candlelight. And the supper is still spareribs and 'risen supe' (rice cooked all day in milk), just as Mother always fixed it, and 'Jule kake' (Norwegian Christmas bread), with red and green jello for dessert. And then, happy companionship about the fire.

"Now as I sit here by the low fire after everyone else has

gone to bed, I like to think of the outdoor beauty of this Christmas Eve, the generous sunlight giving color to the frosty trees.

"Two thousand years since the birth of Jesus, and how far have we come toward freedom? Yet tonight I feel hopeful. The Universe still exists, with all its benevolent attributes. Yes, we have animosity among religious sects, we have tortures mental and physical, we have martyrs. But it seems to me that many people are awakening to the beauty and significance of the universe and what it may mean to us to have better understanding among men. After all, we can be hopeful and grateful and feel more certain, this Christmas, that in time we shall comprehend more intelligently Jesus' teachings. This is a hopeful Christmas."

23

Summer at Moose

§ M · M §

From New Zealand (where again the wapiti, this time trans-planted ones, were the reason for an expedition and seven exciting months for Olaus, Donald, and me); from Norway and Finland; from more trips in Alaska, we nearly always managed to be on the ranch in spring and summer. We felt cheated if we could not be there to watch the thawing of the five-foot banks of snow along our road. (In these later years, with Park Headquarters and the employee's village all moved to Moose, the roads are kept plowed in winter.) The date of the first glimpse of yellow buttercups at the edge of these banks was noted with joy.

The whole parade of plants, animals, and birds goes on from this date, too fast, too many to count, too many keen impressions to chronicle. Yellowbells and purple phacelia by the garden, green grass, green buds everywhere, first robin, first yellow warbler, first sound of ruffed grouse drumming.

Evening is the enchanted time. We always have early dinner, leave the dishes, go out down across the channels over the footbridges to the river, or out the trail to the beaver ponds, skirting the lingering deep snowdrifts in the woods.

By the river will be killdeers and sandpipers running and calling, and mallards, goldeneyes, and mergansers. The beaver may slap his tail at us as we cross the first footbridge, over his channel; nearly always there will be a moose or two or three down in the willows, and at this time of year we may in the evening startle a little band of elk. A few make their way north along this west side of the valley now, and we are always glad to see them here on our acres, for they are after all the reason for our being here living this happy life.

Suddenly we stand still and listen. A ruffed grouse nearby, drumming his love song. Yes, we know which log he is on. Then another—yes, that's the one below the barn. And another —that's the one on the north trail. One spring we counted thirteen. We are always glad to hear each one each spring.

Meanwhile, in the deep dusk, the air is full of the song of white-crowned, Lincoln's, and fox sparrows, of black-headed grosbeak and purple finch and ruby-crowned kinglet. But most thrilling of all, the voice of the woods, the hermit thrush. As we walk back home past the big garden plot, Olaus is sure to say: "We can start the garden in another week."

It would take thousands of words, hundreds of pictures, to tell about the rich variety of life in this river-bottom world along Snake River, and still its spirit could not be captured. It is, so far, an area nearly untouched by man. For our small part of it we are so grateful that through all the years that it was a dude ranch Buster and Frances and their guests were careful never to disturb any wildlife, not even to pick many wild flowers.

So that now, on an afternoon in May, Bob and Mickey and Olaus and I can make our way through the woods and come to a spot where we all kneel and look, and Olaus and Bob take some pictures. Fred, the young artist who lives in one of the cabins, has told us how to find this spot. Under the trees, in thick woods, on shaded mossy ground, a bed of calypso orchids. We count twenty-three: pink, exquisite, and quiet. It is most unusual to find this many in one spot. This is just one of thousands of memories of spring in the river bottom.

Summer is people. People, interesting appreciative ones, in all the cabins. Children and grandchildren in our house. People driving in at all hours of the day. It is great fun; it is pretty strenuous, but we love it.

Every conservationist or friend of a conservationist, every biologist or friend of a biologist, every schoolmate of our three children, or friend of a schoolmate, who happens to be traveling through Jackson Hole will naturally come in to call.

In our first summer on the ranch, when the boys had all come home from war, I suggested to Martin that he put up a sign at the gate: "Headquarters, Tenth Mountain Infantry," since they all seemed to be dropping in. Later it was college friends. Added to these, we had the pleasure of entertaining scientists and students from Norway, Sweden, Finland, India,

Kenya, France, England, Australia, New Zealand, Denmark, South Africa, Canada, and members of the United Nations Secretariat. They all seemed happy to walk in the woods or to swim in our "swimming channel," to talk over all sorts of topics by the fireplace at night. Most of them even enjoyed the sourdough pancakes.

One autumn we had an eminent Swedish scientist as house guest for a few days, and our dear Frances the Chief Ranger's wife and I had planned a large buffet dinner at our house to honor him. That morning Frances and Paul arrived to find Olaus standing in the middle of the kitchen holding a lively white-footed mouse by the nape of the neck and saying to me: "Mardy, will you find a dry can I can put him in?" while our guest, Nils, looked on with an interested smile. I wiped dishwater from my hands, found a can. This was part of one of the experiments Olaus was always carrying on, trapping, marking, and turning loose these mice to see from how far they would return to the same trap. It was a legitimate scientific experiment, later published in a journal, but it sometimes looked strange. Frances said: "Mardy, I'm sorry but we have to go right now if we are going to get the meat for tonight and the other stuff."

I turned to Olaus: "Look, can you pack a lunch for you and Nils for your trip upcountry? There's sandwich stuff in the frig, and here is a whole crate of lovely peaches Ras brought in yesterday. And oh yes, throw out these pancakes to the birds, will you?"

At five o'clock everything was in order, tables set for the

party. I had sort of wondered what kind of sandwiches Olaus had made because the bowl of tunafish filling didn't seem to have been touched, but I was too busy to give it much thought. I was glad to see Olaus and Nils arrive; it was Olaus's habit to go right on working and be changing his clothes while the guests were arriving. Nils came straight to me in the kitchen, face sunburned and beaming: "You know, there is that saying that nothing is so good it couldn't be a little bit better. Today I have had a day which could not possibly be any better! I shall never forget sitting there on the lake looking over at those mountains while we ate lunch; the peaches were delicious, and those pancake sandwiches were the best thing I ever tasted!"

The summer days swept us on like a warm, swiftly flowing stream. If I was lucky, I might get whatever we planned for dinner baked or put together right after breakfast while daughter or daughter-in-law or house guest did the dishes. And if I was still lucky, I could get the bed made and perhaps a few letters typed for Olaus. He, having worked in the garden before breakfast, would be in his study writing, if he was not out in the road or across the road on the picnic ground pouring plaster into some moose or mouse track, or over at the edge of the woods with Mildred getting movies of a sapsucker feeding its young in a hole in an aspen trunk, or out in his studio cabin next door trying to finish a painting.

In any case, I would soon hear whatever grandchildren were playing on the big front porch saying: "Hi! What's your name?" and there would be some visitors; and practically always, after they had left, Olaus would say: "Gosh, those were wonderful people!"

That is how he feels about people, but most of all, about young ones just finding their way. He loves to spend hours with them, and in our years at Moose there have been more and more, coming to ask his advice about careers, about topics for a thesis, about what they can do to help preserve pieces of wilderness they live near or love to hike or climb in. To Olaus, these are the hope, and his chief comfort, and it never matters to him what work is interrupted, what hour of day or night they come.

One morning as I walked to the kitchen to start breakfast, and stopped as usual to look out through the big front windows to the Grand Teton, I called to Olaus: "When you are dressed, will you please go over and see what on earth is going on out on the picnic ground? A red convertible is parked right near the picnic table."

A few moments later: "Well, it's a Kansas license; I saw someone's feet sticking out of the door, and over on the grass there are some lumps in sleeping bags. They're all asleep, whoever they are."

"Kansas, eh? Then it's some of the Bascoms—so it's all right. They'll be over when they wake up."

They were—two sons of a dear doctor friend in Kansas. We never knew when one or two or all four of the sons would roll in to camp somewhere on the place, but it was always a happy occurrence.

Visitors at any hour—coffee on the front porch in midmorning; lunch on the front porch at noon; tea or fruit punch on the porch in late afternoon, and all with homemade cookies. My mother brought me up on the rule that a good housewife always has her cookie jar full. Now when she comes to visit us at Moose she finds herself making one batch after another.

One part of the swiftly moving summer day I insist on. In midafternoon, no matter who comes or goes, I am hiking past the garden, clad in swimsuit and sneakers, and followed by galloping and cavorting grandchildren, all headed toward the swimming channel where a small part of Snake River flows behind an island at the edge of our ranch. The water is cold but caressing, and there is a grassy bank, and low willows, and as you swim you can gaze toward the towering peaks behind the tall spruce forest in the west. I have swum here along with a family of downy-young Barrows's goldeneye ducks and behind a badger who looked like a floating fur rug, and many times near moose unconcernedly crossing the end of the channel. An hour down here, and we are ready for whatever may be waiting back at the house—three more cars in the driveway, unexpected guests for dinner—nothing is too much after that lovely cold Snake River.

Evenings may be quiet, or they may mean thirty-five people for dessert, followed by either Olaus or our friend Mildred showing films, and more talk by the fire.

I have a passion for eating outdoors, and whenever the mosquitoes are not too bad we also have some evenings on the picnic ground; these always include the current population of the ranch, which may be anywhere from fourteen to twenty-four.

Last Fourth of July we gathered for an evening picnic and Bob and Mickey joined us. We had no fireworks, but we had fellowship and good food. And we had music—for as it grew dark and we all sat closer to the fire, there came from the woods very near at hand a trimuphant rising and soaring and yip-yipping song of coyotes. And while they were still singing, out of the woods at the other side walked a cow moose, then a calf, then a bull with budding antlers. They strolled by, stopped to chew on some young firs, stood and gazed at us— uninvited but welcome guests at our Fourth of July observance.

Most of our summer evenings are quiet—the grandchildren in bed, their parents glad to sit by the fire (in a log house, even summer nights are cool). At his table at the back of the room, Olaus will be still working, writing or sketching. The rest of us will be reading, or wrangling quietly over a Double-Crostic in the *Saturday Review*. Suddenly Joanne or Martin or someone else will lift his eyes from a book: "Listen! There they are."

"Yes, they're really singing tonight." Coyotes.

Or maybe not. Maybe this time it is great horned owls, in the tall dead perching tree beyond the woodshed: "Whoo-hoo-hoo—hoo, hoo."

These two sounds are all we usually hear at night. We know the woods around us are full of all kinds of life, but they are quiet at night.

All except one or two species. Some nights we are awakened by a thump or a crash outside the kitchen. Maybe it is only the pet marten finding a tidbit left on the bird shelf attached to the kitchen window. Another crash. Something bigger than a marten.

One night last summer I put on robe and slippers and went out to see. I turned on the kitchen light. There with front forearms akimbo on the bird tray stood a big brown bear. I went over and leaned arms akimbo on the counter and we regarded each other, just the window glass between us. She was unusual; she had a band of fawn color right across her nose. She was blinking her eyes, as though to say: "Turn off that light; it bothers me."

"Well, what do you want?" I finally said. "You'd better go on somewhere else. There's nothing to eat here."

I watched her clumsily hoist herself off and disappear in the dark, and went back to bed thinking: "What a great place to live!"

I was delighted when Olaus left government service and plunged with all his might into a more challenging, freer task. But at the same time I am eternally grateful to government service, first for sending Olaus to Alaska, where we met, and then for sending us to Jackson Hole, our wapiti wilderness.

And to this life at Moose the wapiti led us.

24

The Valley Now

§ M · M §

Some day a social scientist is going to have a great time working out the sociology of Jackson Hole. In the meantime Olaus and I and our friends have discussed it in front of the fireplace on many an evening.

All the modern conveniences, including television and airplane service and a big luxury hotel at Moran, have come to Jackson Hole. But why? The reason for all of it is still the place itself, the untouched natural part of it. There is indeed, as we have all been saying through the years, "something about it."

Why do so many of the young people who grow up here go away, get some training or get jobs, and then come back? Our young friends say it could be two things. One: because they grow up in a non-competitive environment here, the outside world is just too difficult for them. It is easier to come home; one can always make some kind of living, the folks are here, and the friends of childhood and the beautiful familiar surroundings.

Two: the simple, free, relaxed atmosphere here, and all the loved outdoor activities, mean more in a life than money, even for those who have proven their ability in the otuside world. They too come back.

And that brings us to skiing.

One autumn we had as weekend guests a charming young couple from Norway. He is a paleobotanist, or palinologist, as the new word goes, and in his year over here had been offered four different, very lucrative jobs in oil research. But if they decided to stay in the United States the job would have to be near a ski area, for, as they said to us solemnly: "We cannot live without skiing."

As Dorothy, our doctor's wife, and herself a skier, says: "It's a disease," and this expresses what many feel.

In Jackson Hole we have skiing through a long winter season, and in addition hiking, climbing, swimming, canoeing, fishing through the glorious sunny summers. Perhaps this alone explains a phenomenon we have noted in recent years. We can count quite a few young people, and older ones too, who have given up the profession or activity for which they were trained, and taken up something entirely different, so they could live in Jackson Hole and raise their children here.

An oil geologist runs a sporting-goods store, another geologist a printing shop, a television expert runs a book and camera

shop, doctors who could make more money as specialists elsewhere prefer to stay in general practice here, and young lawyers follow the same pattern. A man who was highly paid as a commercial photographer in Illinois prefers to live here and work at anything to make a living. The list could go on. And some wealthy people who could of course live anywhere on the planet have made permanent homes here.

In a way, all these are the New Wave in the valley, and there is one outstanding feature about them: they appreciate the valley for its own sake; they will want to cherish its natural values.

And now, perhaps because of this New Wave of the last decade, Culture has reared its head in Jackson Hole. We no longer offer only *Clover the Killer* and the *Cache Creek Posse* every night at the Town Square. We have the Jackson Hole Fine Arts Festival—symphony concerts, two a week; chamber music; the Laubins doing their incomparable Indian dances; a foreign-film series; an art exhibit; and a folk-song festival.

Some of us were skeptical in the beginning. Why would Eastern visitors who could hear the very best symphonies all winter want to bother to attend symphonies here? They didn't come West for this; they came for Western flavor, for riding, and fishing and singing by a campfire. But one day Betty set me straight on this: "Why think only of the dudes? What about us who live here and never get to hear or see symphony orchestras? Why shouldn't the local population enjoy this, or be educated to enjoy it? There are more and more folks living here now who do want such things."

And that is the way it works out. The Fine Arts Festival is now a virile organism, thanks to the generosity of a few in the beginning, and to their hard work and to the skill and talents they have been able to bring here. It is apparently not difficult now to recruit a full orchestra made up of members of great orchestras all over the United States. They have a paid vacation in the Tetons; they give lessons to local pupils if they wish. They want to come.

There is of course a great contrast in the material realities of living between the time we came here and today, with the new, fully modern homes in the valley. One pioneer ranch woman said to me:

"They can talk about the good old days, and of course I'm glad I lived through it all, but how many of us would want to go back to it now? A lot of these folks have maybe forgotten how it was to be on a ranch where we crawled out before daylight, lit kerosene lamps and built three wood fires, and shoveled a way to the barn, milked five cows and harnessed a team to a sleigh and took the kids three miles to school and came back and hurried to get all the chores done before dark. Maybe carrying water from a creek, maybe pumping a hand pump in the kitchen; heating wash water in a boiler on the range; carrying all the slops out in buckets; scrubbing clothes on a washboard. And then mending them at night by a kerosene lamp when you were so dead beat you could hardly lift a needle! We didn't have time to gaze much at the Tetons, I can tell you!"

Nowadays, Park Service employees and ranch people alike live in fully electric, three- or four-bedroom homes—wall-to-wall carpet, two ovens, heated garage for the car or two cars, children picked up by a school bus a few yards from the door. The maintenance crew comes to clean even the driveway with a baby snowplow, clothes go into the automatic washer and are lifted out forty-five minutes later; milk and cream are delivered at the door. If mending still has to be done by hand, it can be done while watching a good television program.

One question pops into my mind. Where is the happy middle ground between the old-time ranch wife who was so pressed by arduous physical tasks that she was numbed to the glories of her environment, and the modern housewife so engrossed with gadgets that she may not *take* time to gaze at the Tetons? This is an interesting thought, and to me it brings the realization that we have lived through one era in Jackson Hole and into another.

Perhaps to the real Old-timers the early 1900's were a golden age of independence from the outer world. To those of us who lived at Moose in the early 1940's—the earlier years of Grand Teton National Park—that was a golden age too: a group small enough to gather together in one small recreation hall, large enough so there was talent for many kinds of fun and good fellowship, all handmade and home-created.

In those winters Olaus and I were glad to ski the mile to the highway, drive three miles to Park Headquarters, change from ski clothes to dancing clothes at the Chief Ranger's house, dance and sing and laugh and eat until one in the morning; change clothes again, drive back to Moose, park the car, get on our skis and ski home, alive in every cell and so thankful to be there and among those wonderful companions. It was such a good life that we knew it with every fiber of our being, and felt immensely fortunate.

But through every era and every "golden age," the core, the reason for it all, is the place itself, the spiritual impact, conscious or unconscious, of the valley itself.

Yes, the highways are broader, smoother; the dude ranches more comfortable; the museums and visitors' centers too much like modern buildings anywhere else; the campgrounds more extensive; and signs too numerous. But leave your car, walk away from the highway anywhere in Jackson Hole, and there is the quiet world of nature as John Colter, Beaver Dick, and Al Austin knew it.

I hope it will be a long long time before man can spoil it all. We shall go on with the little concerns of life, but the mountains are there, and now and then we may stop and look up. And if the valley itself can be cherished, there may be one "golden age" after another—for our grandchildren and their grandchildren. Some of them may go to the moon, but perhaps the valley of the Tetons will still be a place of return and enchantment.

As for us, we are thankful to have lived here through one era and into another.

25

Autumn

{{ O·M }}

I have often tried to catch the exact time that autumn comes. Presumably it is the first of August—according to the calendar. And the calendar is probably right. Sometime, while still reveling in summer's greenery, you ride along a mountain trail and casually notice a willow branch that has turned a pale yellow. It seems an accident. Surely summer isn't over! You just won't believe it. Why, it was only a few weeks ago that we were looking forward to the first green of spring. Of course, see—the landscape is still green. It's still summer.

But the thought will not leave. You begin to notice that many early blooms have gone—plants are going to seed. The tall larkspur has lost its freshness; the blue flowers have given way to fat seedpods, and some of these are ripening. If you come cautiously to a mountain meadow, you may see a band of elk feeding. They are picking here and there as they move along, systematically snipping off the ripening pods of the larkspur. In spring this green plant is poisonous to them, and unlike the cattle, they seem to know it. Now they relish its seeds. The lupine too is in pod, and then you notice that the geranium is going to seed. Some of its leaves have turned red along the edges. The season of fruition has arrived.

An artist friend remarked to me on one August day: "And autumn will be here soon, and then we'll all go crazy!"

His remark is justified by the march of colors as the season grows upon us. All through September the display is on, and even in October; perhaps the deepest tones are reached then. The floor of the aspen groves is strewn with yellow leaves. If you dare to walk through the enchanted place, you almost hold your breath. The gold reaches in, with golden thoughts.

In September 1932 I was camped high on the slopes of Sheep Mountain. I find this note in my journal, the part of the journal not concerned with strictly scientific data: "Yesterday was blustery and cold on Sheep Mt., with bank after bank of angry clouds rolling up from the southwest, with a warning sputter of snow or large drops of rain. After a long hard day on the high mesas, observing sheep, shivering in the cold wind, I had stumbled down the rocky slopes to my camp below, grateful for a tent and a fire and food. This morning I awoke to find the stars fading in the pale glow of a clear dawn and presently looked out from my sleeping bag to see the Tetons flooded with bright light.

"This is the season when the first frosts have nipped the

vegetation, set the fireweed ablaze, reddened the geraniums, lightly brushed the pine grass with tints of soft yellow, with maroon over the deep basal green. But the aspens are still green and in all the protected hollows and in the shelter of the pines there is the green exuberance of summer even yet. After all, Jack Frost has only made his first dab at the landscape. It is at such a time that birds are flocking, summer cares long over, and the abundance of harvest time at hand. Chipmunks are reveling in a wealth of grass seeds, ripening berries, snowberry, serviceberry, and other fruits. These first cold nights set the birds a-wing on long, strong flights, such as the nutcracker flying over my tent this morning. And how noisy they are! 'Kraah, kraah, kraah!' A harsh call, but somehow pleasing, so vigorous and fearless it sounds.

"From my perch on this great lichen-covered boulder on the hill, I can look down into Jackson Hole and see here and there the geometrical plots of fields. There is a faint droning sound, sometimes I imagine the sound of an automobile—the hum of humankind. There lies civilization, of a sort. Along the base of the Tetons hangs a low dense cloudbank, lead color below, silvery above. Below that fog the people are no doubt unaware of the brilliance of a bright early morning on the heights.

"Here, in the grateful warmth of sunlight dissolving the frost from the grass, I hear the bark of a squirrel, the call of a raven. A chipmunk runs almost over my feet in his happy search for breakfast; from the woods across the ravine comes a tap-tap of cones dropped by a squirrel from high in a white-bark pine, a medley of chirps and calls, the miscellaneous sounds of a woodland busy at breakfast. High up, there under the rising sun and above timberline, lies the grassy mesa where live the mountain sheep, rarely disturbed by any intrusion."

We were driving up the valley just north of town one evening later in the fall, a group of us going to dinner at the Turner's Triangle X Ranch. The landscape had reached that special stage of autumn hue with pale gold grass, maroon of willows, and the variegated reds and browns and old rose on the foothills over toward Sheep Mountain. The sun, lowering over the Tetons, cast a smoldering intensity over the pattern. It almost made us gasp. Fortunately no one spoke, but I wanted to reach out to the driver and say: "Stop! I want all that! I want to do something about it. I can't get enough just looking at it like this!"

Nearly always autumn in Jackson Hole comes in two chapters. First those burnished golden days in early September, when there is in the air a feeling of the end of a season coming on. In the hills the wapiti are busy with their wooing; in the foothills and in the valley the small animals are busy storing winter food, all the rich harvest of summer's bounty. At the same time the summer visitors are beginning to leave. Some dude ranches are being closed up and put away for the winter, caretakers arranged for, to be the sole winter occupants. A period of taking stock, making an accounting. In these perfect blue-and-gold days those who have to leave now for school or business have been packing their bags, at dude ranches, in the campgrounds, and leaving by plane or bus or car.

The valley will be quieter. But for those who are staying, there is a glorious second autumn coming. Nearly every year it comes, this second glory, after an interlude of storm and rain, and cold, and new snow on the mountaintops. Each time we have forgotten; each time we are surprised. Now the air is full of cobwebs, the trees stand tall and waiting, partly bare of leaves; tall yellow grasses are infinitely still; there is no breeze. The sun shines warm, the sky is the epitome of blue, wild roses and hawthorn bushes are red flames in front of the evergreens.

We feel a surprised gratitude. We had been thinking of winter joys to come, but, oh my, we are glad to hang on to autumn a little longer! And sometimes this goes on for weeks. We all move about at our fall chores as though in a warm golden dream. A time to get everything ready for winter, a time for the ranches which stay open for the hunting season to be putting summer equipment away and getting the hunting gear ready.

And a time for all the natives who have been separated by summer's demands of guests and visitors to get together again for a picnic, or a hike, or a cozy chat by the fire of an evening; a time of reunion. Now we have the hours to enjoy the valley ourselves in leisurely fashion, to visit again our favorite lakes and canyons before the snow comes. I really think this may be the season those of us who live here love most deeply. It is like a benediction.

Our old friends Sunny and Esther, and Mardy and I, have the same wedding anniversary date in August. But in August we are all too taken up with summer visitors and all the busy chores to get together. So we have picked October 19 as our date, and then we take a picnic lunch and go up to the north part of Jackson Lake, and for hours we roam the beach and bask in the sun. Esther is looking for arrowheads; I am looking for most anything else, especially tracks in the wet sand.

But in the afternoon I have left the rest of them for a bit, and am roaming in the forest along Pilgrim Creek, feeling again the benediction of October as I walk through the woods among the bronze cottonwoods and white-trunked aspens, glimpsing the blue mountains through the foliage as a few golden leaves come fluttering down on the trunks.

The dying year? I feel it is only adulthood, a prodigal sowing of seed, storing for the future, planning for the future —culmination of the work of the year.

As I stand and watch a squirrel hurrying by with a cone in his mouth, I remember a paragraph Mardy had been reading to me from A. S. M. Hutchinson's novel *If Winter Comes:*

"Nature was to him in October, and not in spring, poignantly suggestive, deeply mysterious, in her intense and visible occupation. She was enormously busy, but she was serenely busy. She was stripping her house of its deckings, dismantling her habitation to the last and uttermost leaf; but she stripped, dismantled, extinguished, broke away, not in despair, defeat, but in ordered preparation and with exquisite certitude of glory anew. . . . October spoke to him of Nature's sublime imperviousness to doubt; of her enormous certainty, old as creation, based in sure foundations of the world. 'Take down. It is beginning.' "

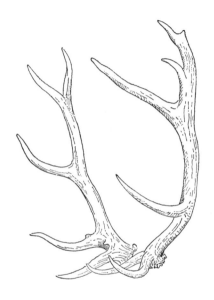

A Note about the Authors

OLAUS J. MURIE (1889–1963) was born in Moorhead, Minnesota. He received his B.A. (and an honorary D.Sc.) from Pacific University and a M.S. from the University of Michigan. Mr. Murie's fieldwork as a biologist took him to the most remote wilderness areas of North America, first on an exploration of Hudson Bay for the Carnegie Museum, then to the wilds of Labrador, and successively to the Aleutians, British Columbia, and repeatedly to Alaska. From 1920 to 1946, Murie was field biologist for the U. S. Biological Survey (now the Fish and Wildlife Service) and during those years and after made his famous studies of the life history of the elk. He was a director (from 1946) and then president (1950–7) of the Wilderness Society and was the recipient of numerous conservation society awards, among them the Pugsley Bronze Medal (1954), the Audubon Medal (1959), and the Aldo Leopold Memorial Award (1952). Olaus Murie was the author of *The Elk in North America*, *A Field Guide to Animal Tracks*, and other books and monographs on coyotes, bears, caribou, and other large mammals. He was a frequent contributor of articles on natural history to various professional journals and illustrated his own books and articles and those of other writers with remarkably atmospheric pen-and-ink sketches.

MARGARET E. MURIE was born in Seattle, Washington. She attended the public schools in Fairbanks, Alaska, spent two years at Reed College in Oregon, one year at Simmons College in Boston, and was the first woman graduate of the University of Alaska. Two months after her graduation she married Olaus Murie and through the years worked closely with him in his wildlife studies, often accompanying him on his field trips. Mrs. Murie is the author of *Two in the Far North* and has contributed articles to various magazines, including *Natural History* and *The Living Wilderness*. Mrs. Murie, who has three grown children, makes her home in Moose, Wyoming.

October 1965

A Note on the Type

The text of this book is set in Monticello, a Linotype revival of the original Binny & Ronaldson Roman No. 1, cut by Archibald Binny and cast in 1796 by that Philadelphia type foundry. The face was named Monticello in honor of its use in the monumental fifty-volume *Papers of Thomas Jefferson*, published by Princeton University Press. Monticello is a transitional type design, embodying certain features of Bulmer and Baskerville, but it is a distinguished face in its own right.